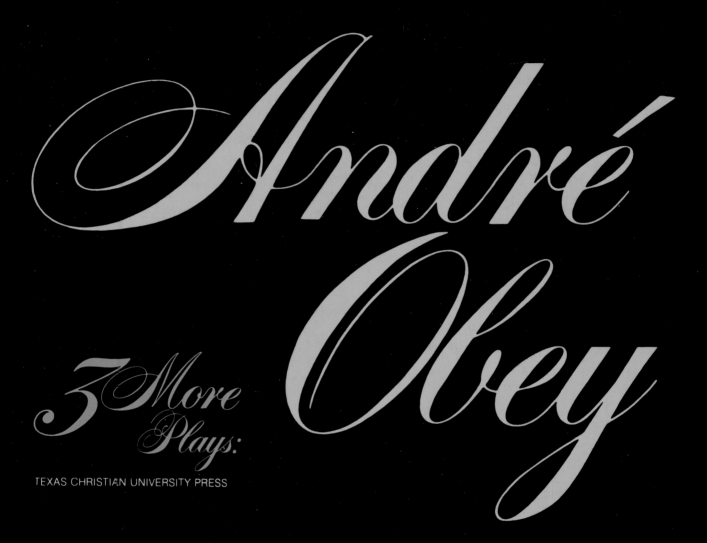

André Obey

3 More Plays:

TEXAS CHRISTIAN UNIVERSITY PRESS

André Obey

3 More Plays:

THE REUNION
MOSES AND THE MOUNTAIN
THE WINDOW

Translated from the French by

Judith D. Suther and Earle D. Clowney

THE TEXAS CHRISTIAN UNIVERSITY PRESS, FORT WORTH, TEXAS

FIRST PRINTING
Copyright© 1977 by Texas Christian University Press

Library of Congress Catalog Card No. 76-52768
Manufactured in the United States of America

Despite Monsieur Obey's deteriorating health during the last months of his life, he and Madame Obey were generous in their encouragement of these translations. We hope Madame Obey will accept this book as a tribute to the memory of her husband, who died on April 11, 1975, at their country estate near Saumur, France.

Appreciation is also due to Frank Jones, who made some very helpful suggestions on the translation of *The Reunion* and *The Window*.

André Obey at the Obeys' country estate in Saumur, France.

Foreword

The plays in this volume represent a more definitive statement on André Obey's theatre than was originally intended. Obey's death as the manuscript approached its final form suddenly put a stamp of finality on the lines. *The Reunion*, which had its première in the French version in 1973, can now be listed as Obey's last play to be performed during his lifetime. *Moses and the Mountain*, completed in 1969, ranks in its author's judgment as one of his best; *Moses* is sure to invite comparison with *Noah*, the showpiece from Obey's earlier years. *The Window*, a one-act play written in 1959, we add as a sample of Obey's shorter pieces and for the current appeal of its subject matter. Joan of Arc is once again a favored figure.

Like the three plays in our previous volume of translations, these reaffirm the vitality of inherited patterns in dramatic art. It is now beyond dispute that Obey's mode is the neoclassical. His creative imagination thrives on the transformation of the complex and contradictory matter of legend into new statements. *The Reunion* reflects his lifelong immersion in *The Odyssey* and his vision of the personal tragedy of Ulysses and Penelope. *Moses and the Mountain* uses the material of the Old Testament to assess the relation of God to man, a relation which Obey sees as desperately one-sided. *The Window*, an unpretentious play about Joan in which Joan is not a character, re-enacts the day of May 30, 1431, in the life of a modest Norman family whose house overlooks the town square of Rouen.

Obey's faith in the *tréteau nu* (bare stage) of Jacques Copeau could not be better illustrated than by these plays. All of them can be performed against a neutral background, with the barest of props. While *The Window* is more specific than the other two in its description of the required set, an inventive scenic designer will have no trouble representing the window itself by a simple frame and the door leading downstairs by an equally schematic arrangement. The primacy of the text, a principle Obey practices from his early years with the Compagnie des Quinze to *The Reunion*, makes his plays accessible to theatre groups of the most limited financial means. We have rendered the French into English with all the faithfulness we could manage, while lending an ear to the playable qualities of the language.

Through all these plays runs the thread of compassion for simple people caught in the net of fate. As a humanizer of gods and heroes, Obey knows few equals. Whoever has heard his Agamemnon and Iphigenia, his Noah, his Don Juan remembers them. We offer this volume so that English-speaking readers and playgoers may have a taste of his Ulysses and Penelope, his Moses, and his Joan of Lorraine.

Judith D. Suther
Seattle, Washington

Earle D. Clowney
Atlanta, Georgia

January, 1976

2

The Reunion

LE JOUR DU RETOUR

Characters, in order of appearance:

Eurycleia, Nurse
First Maidservant
Second Maidservant
Philoetius, Chief cowherd
Eumaeus, Chief swineherd
Penelope
Ulysses

"In short, one can say that Homer's poems are nothing other than dramas."
— Pseudo-Plutarch, *Life of Homer*

The Reunion

The bedroom of Ulysses' house, on Ithaca. Three doors: one, at the back, opens onto the corridor; another, on the right, leads into the bathroom; a third, on the left, opens into Penelope's apartment.
It is autumn. Evening is setting in.
As the lights come up, two young maidservants, in high spirits, are making the bed and whispering excitedly. Seated in a small, low armchair, Eurycleia, the nurse, watches them.

EURYCLEIA: All right, girls, let's get a move on! Watch what you're doing. A little less talk and a little more work!

FIRST MAIDSERVANT: We may be talk-

*Play in two acts with no curtain

ing, Nurse, but we're working.

EURYCLEIA: Not the way you'd work if you kept your mouths shut. Or go ahead, talk, but talk about your work.

SECOND MAIDSERVANT: That's just what we're doing, Madam. We were discussing how to make the bed.

FIRST MAIDSERVANT: *(Emphatically)* The bed of the reunited couple . . .

SECOND MAIDSERVANT: . . . reunited after a separation of twenty years. That's something worth special notice, don't you think? Almost a wedding night!

(Short pause)

EURYCLEIA: They weren't really separated.

FIRST MAIDSERVANT: What do you mean, not really separated?

EURYCLEIA: They had such confidence

in each other, although they were hundreds of miles apart, that for them, every night, it was as if they were touching each other.

SECOND MAIDSERVANT: Except they *weren't* touching each other.

FIRST MAIDSERVANT: They were far from touching each other.

SECOND MAIDSERVANT: Very far. Now if I had a husband . . .

FIRST MAIDSERVANT: . . . yes, I'd touch him all day long, to be sure he was really there, that I still had him.

SECOND MAIDSERVANT: Yes, that he wasn't fooling around somewhere with another woman. Men are always slipping through your fingers, you know.

FIRST MAIDSERVANT: You can say that again! Take your eye off him for a second, a single second, and ffuitt!, disappeared. You can always run catch him, though.

EURYCLEIA: You're not going to compare our Master and his wife to yourselves and your playmates, I hope?

FIRST MAIDSERVANT: That's just why we're discussing how to make their bed.

SECOND MAIDSERVANT: What was this bed like when they used it every night? Maybe you know that, Nurse?

FIRST MAIDSERVANT: And how did they use it? That's the point: to sleep in or to make love in?

SECOND MAIDSERVANT: Or both, alternating?

FIRST MAIDSERVANT: Master looks to me like a . . . a real wolf.

EURYCLEIA: Hold your tongue, you shameless wench!

FIRST MAIDSERVANT: It's funny, everybody talked about him all the time and I didn't even know him.

SECOND MAIDSERVANT: Me either. Well, I mean I barely knew him. I have a very vague memory of the day he left for the war. I was just a kid, I think I was five or six years old. Everybody was in the courtyard crying. I remember clearly that everybody was crying. I was too, like everybody else, without knowing exactly why. Master and Mistress were standing on the steps. In each other's arms. I slipped up little by little to the first row, in front of the steps. Nobody said anything to me. I watched them with my greedy little eyes. Ever since I was a kid, love has always been my favorite subject. I remember, I remember . . . All of a sudden, just before he left, Master whispered something to Mistress. For years and years I wondered what in the world he could have said to that beautiful, sobbing woman. And I must say it was only a short while ago that I found the answer. They went back into the house. Outside, everybody stopped crying, one after another. Several people even smiled, a little sadly, but they smiled. Do you remember that, Madam Eurycleia?

EURYCLEIA: *(With emotion)* Of course, oh! Of course!

SECOND MAIDSERVANT: Master and Mistress were gone a long time. I was very young, I was thinking about something else when Master came back out and looked at us with eyes that saw nothing. He called for his chariot, jumped in it with a single leap, and took off at a fast trot. If you'd told me I wouldn't see him for twenty years! Mistress came out a few minutes later, very pale. "Where is he?" she cried, "Where is he?" Nobody answered. In the distance you could hear the noise of wheels on the road and the mules' bells. An old memory, yes, a twenty-year-old memory . . . Well! All Master had to do was look at me, just now . . .

FIRST MAIDSERVANT: He looked at both of us. One after the other, like this (She imitates.), gliding back and forth, restless. A real caress. And then, it's strange, my legs . . .

SECOND MAIDSERVANT: Mine too! My legs started shaking. Even though he's not young anymore.

FIRST MAIDSERVANT: No, he's not, and when he passed me in the corridor, he was still covered with dust and dried blood. I think he's a man that women can't . . .

EURYCLEIA: (Interrupting her) That's enough, that's enough! You wretched gossips. Do you actually think this kind of thing is your business? Your indiscretion knows no bounds!

SECOND MAIDSERVANT: I don't agree. Ever since I started working here, I've always been taught to speak freely.

EURYCLEIA: Well, you shouldn't have been. In my time . . .

FIRST MAIDSERVANT: (Exasperated) Here come the stories from the good old days!

SECOND MAIDSERVANT: (To Eurycleia) Take us as we are. Everybody knows that for twenty years, since the war, the world has changed course and nothing is the way it used to be. But just because we

call things by their names doesn't mean we're indiscreet.

FIRST MAIDSERVANT: Exactly! Or promiscuous either. (Changing the subject) So, how do we make the bed?

SECOND MAIDSERVANT: Well, that depends.

FIRST MAIDSERVANT: Depends on what?

SECOND MAIDSERVANT: Uh, on the . . . the position . . . on who'll ride and who'll be ridden, the man or the woman.

FIRST MAIDSERVANT: (Short laugh) Ha ha! And who do you think it'll be? Master or his wife?

EURYCLEIA: (Indignant) Oh!

SECOND MAIDSERVANT: I have no idea. How do people make love at their age? You must know how they do it, Nurse?

EURYCLEIA: (Stammering with indignation) What I know . . . what . . . what I know is that I nursed Ulysses when he was a baby and that . . . that when I was nursing him, love, or what you call love, didn't bother him at all.

FIRST MAIDSERVANT: Oh! He must have started early.

EURYCLEIA: (Furious) That will do, my girl. Not another word on this subject, I'm warning you!

(Silence. The two maidservants make the bed, consulting each other in lowered voices. Philoetius, the chief cowherd, enters from the back. He walks slowly, lost in thought.)

Ah, there you are! What's happening? You look awful!

PHILOETIUS: It's because the job I've

just finished wasn't pretty. No, really not pretty. Can I sit down?

EURYCLEIA: *(Sharply)* Certainly not! Not before you scrub yourself clean and brush your clothes. You're as dirty as . . .

THE TWO MAIDSERVANTS: *(Together)* . . . a pig! *(They laugh.)*

EURYCLEIA: *(To Philoetius)* And don't lean on the wall. The paint soils easily, you know.

PHILOETIUS: *(Glum)* How about the floor? I'm beat.

EURYCLEIA: The floor's all right, if you want to sit there. *(Philoetius lets himself down heavily and heaves a sigh of relief.)*

PHILOETIUS: Ouf! That's better. I've been on my feet since five o'clock this morning. What a day, old girl, what a day!

EURYCLEIA: Yes. I think it'll figure in the history of this house.

PHILOETIUS: And not only this house: dozens of others with it. All those men dead, just imagine! All of them dead.

(The two maidservants have stopped working.)

FIRST MAIDSERVANT: Did he really kill them all?

PHILOETIUS: Kill them? You can say that again. And every one of them dead as a doornail. Me and my herdsmen and some of the maidservants, we dragged a good hundred of them to the back of the courtyard and dumped them in a pile.

SECOND MAIDSERVANT: A . . . a hundred?

PHILOETIUS: Oh, yeah, easy. I didn't count them, but my head herdsman did, and he told me there was exactly a hundred and nine.

SECOND MAIDSERVANT: A hundred and nine guys exterminated! The cream of the city!

FIRST MAIDSERVANT: They deserved it.

SECOND MAIDSERVANT: I'm not denying that, but . . . Philoetius, are you sure nobody will take it out on Master?

PHILOETIUS: Absolutely sure. Nobody would dare. Master, as you call him, is the king of this country. The way I hear it, he has the protection of the gods and he commands an army of the most loyal servants.

FIRST MAIDSERVANT: Loyal? Loyal? I could name you a good hundred of them that are traitors.

PHILOETIUS: The traitors are now part of the hundred and nine burning at the back of the courtyard.

EURYCLEIA: You burned them?

PHILOETIUS: What else can you do? They're roasted by now. You should have seen the smoke! *(He yawns.)* Ah! I'm drunk with corpses. Me and my men were really rushed for time, you know what I mean? The boss said to me, "Get rid of that for me!" So we piled them all up on top of each other like firewood for winter. If you could have seen the mountain that makes, over a hundred corpses! And all of them scowling.

EURYCLEIA: Scowling?

PHILOETIUS: Oh, yeah. They all got furious just as they were dying and their faces twisted and got all deformed by hate, or rage. They won't let go. Because they were cut down by a savage death, they'll never

6

be appeased. All of them are pale, I mean pale as death. And there are wounds in that pile — hideous! That's all I'll tell you. *(Short pause)*

FIRST MAIDSERVANT: How did it happen?

SECOND MAIDSERVANT: Tell us about it!

PHILOETIUS: *(Weary)* Oh! . . . *(He makes a vague gesture.)*

EURYCLEIA: Of course you'll tell us! You were there. You saw everything.

PHILOETIUS: Maybe I saw everything, but not like I see you there now. There was a kind of . . . of fog between my eyes and the . . . and the . . .

EURYCLEIA: Massacre?

PHILOETIUS: That's it, massacre. A frightful massacre. Good God! What a slaughter. I got dizzy seeing them fall. It made me sick.

EURYCLEIA: You didn't do a little massacring yourself?

PHILOETIUS: Oh, sure! Why should I hide from it? I struck a few blows with my master Ulysses, his son Telemachus and the swineherd Eumaeus. At first we were careful what we did. There wasn't any hurry, and Ulysses had made room for us with a volley of arrows. For awhile I even had time to see who I was killing. It was Pisandrus. With a pike right in his chest. *(Reflecting)* Pisandrus, yes . . . *(To Eurycleia)* Have you ever seen a man die?

EURYCLEIA: Certainly I have, but not like that.

PHILOETIUS: It's a . . . a grandiose feeling. You have a guy that wants nothing better than to live, who's even living twice, all strained and taut as a bow. You have a feeling, all of a sudden, that you've known him forever, like nobody has ever known him before. He's standing there, swollen with strength, bursting with energy. You're sure that any second he's going to know you too, completely, down to the core. You face each other, with hate. You stammer out insults, you splutter with rage and your arm, the one that's holding the javelin, cries out, voiceless from inside you: "Well, go on! What are you waiting for?" And you go on. Suddenly. *(He gets up and acts out the scene.)* You jump at the first chance you get. In a tenth of a second, when his eye flinches a little or his arm, the one holding the sword, starts to quiver before the attack. Hah! In a flash, you leap into the hole that opens up under your javelin. You shout: "Hah!"

FIRST MAIDSERVANT: *(As if hypnotized)* Hah!

PHILOETIUS: *(Laughing)* Look at her! And the other one too, see? They're killing Pisandrus.

EURYCLEIA: Until they become mothers, girls love war, that's a known fact. *(To Philoetius)* And then what? Go on.

PHILOETIUS: With a sort of pleasure I can't describe, I felt the iron of my javelin go into the guy, very easy, like into butter. I said to myself, "I have him!" And I had him. It was the guy's sword that fell first. It fell on the flagstones ringing like a bell. Bong! Then the guy . . . Pisandrus, yes, he fell too while his blood was gushing out of him like some sort of fury. Then a sort of veil came down over his face, like he was going blind in a second. The whole thing is etched into me. I saw it clearly, he was the first one . . . Pisandrus, yes. The Master, nearby, shouted to me: "Great hit!" I looked for another guy to kill. My head was already spinning.

SECOND MAIDSERVANT: But still, with your cattle, you must be used to it.

PHILOETIUS: That's got nothing to do with it. With cattle, it's mechanical—a blow with the mallet, always the same, in the middle of the forehead, and the steer falls on his knees. And if you catch his eye, you see there's nothing behind it. But a man . . . a bad man . . . one of those bad men that was guzzling and gorging on our place, like Ulysses' house was their own house — thunder and lightning! *(Short pause)* The second one I hit was named Ctesippus.

EURYCLEIA: I know him.

SECOND MAIDSERVANT: We do too!

FIRST MAIDSERVANT: Only too well!

SECOND MAIDSERVANT: From too close up! Every time you passed him in a corridor, he managed to mash you against the wall, as if the corridor was too narrow for two to pass side by side. And then . . .

FIRST MAIDSERVANT: Yes, you really would have thought he had six hands, you could feel them running everywhere on you. *(She shivers.)* Brrr!

PHILOETIUS: I struck him down with pleasure. He was a crude type. When we still thought Ulysses was a beggar, taken in through charity, he sent him a steer's hoof at the dinner table, or rather he threw it at him like an insult, and it missed the Master's head by a hair and went banging into the wall behind him. If he had ever touched him, I think Telemachus would have deprived me of the pleasure of killing him.

SECOND MAIDSERVANT: How did you kill this one?

FIRST MAIDSERVANT: *(Avidly)* Yes, yes, tell us everything!

PHILOETIUS: I don't remember exactly. You don't pay attention to any but the first guy you bring down, you know. After that, it's just . . . you feel caught up in a sort of . . . routine.

EURYCLEIA: A routine, already? With the second victim? It must be a trade that can be learned fast.

PHILOETIUS: What? Killing your fellow man? Yes, I think we have it in our blood. Take Eumaeus, you know him well. Good old Eumaeus, the chief swineherd? You remember him when one of his pigs was being bled for the table, one crop more and he would have burst out crying. Well, I wish you could have seen him a couple of hours ago, massacring a guy named Polybus. Such deliberate movements, such calm, such strength! My word, I wouldn't have liked to be in the place of that Polybus. He scared me.

FIRST MAIDSERVANT: *(Incredulous)* Eumaeus?!

PHILOETIUS: That's right.

(Enter Eumaeus from the right.)

EUMAEUS: What did Eumaeus do?

EURYCLEIA: It seems that you fought like a lion.

EUMAEUS: I don't know how lions fight when they're furious, but it's true I was furious. Look *(He holds out his hands.),* I'm still shaking.

PHILOETIUS: What about the boss?

EUMAEUS: Oh, him! Furious or not, nobody could tell. It all happens on the inside. He lets nothing show but just what he wants, when he wants, how he wants. He's an astounding man!

EURYCLEIA: Oh, you can say that again!

EUMAEUS: God knows I've thought about him all the time he was gone! Every day, several times a day and even sometimes at night when a nightmare would wake me up with the idea he was dead. Well, yesterday when I saw him again, I didn't even recognize him. I can't explain it to you. He . . . he didn't look like himself, I mean not at all. He was much better than the memory I had of him.

EURYCLEIA: That's because he had suffered. Twenty years of suffering makes a difference. That turns you into a man.

EUMAEUS: Yes . . . that must be it. *(Sudden burst of joy)* But what luck, old friends, that he came back, how about that! What wonderful luck!

EURYCLEIA AND PHILOETIUS: *(Warmly)* Yes, yes! Oh, yes!

EUMAEUS: Now that we have him back, the travels are over, eh? He won't leave anymore!

EURYCLEIA: No! We won't let him!

EUMAEUS: These girls aren't saying anything. Don't they agree?

FIRST MAIDSERVANT: We don't know him very well.

SECOND MAIDSERVANT: *(Enthusiastically)* But all we ask is to know him better.

EURYCLEIA: Hold on, girls! *(To Eumaeus, ironically)* They have already come under the influence of his charm, so they say. It made them — how was it? — it made their legs shake. Their legs shake! Imagine that.

EUMAEUS: *(Laughing)* They're not the only ones! From Troy to Ithaca, for twenty years, there must have been plenty of legs shaking!

(Philoetius laughs with him.)

EURYCLEIA: Enough on this subject.

PHILOETIUS: Just one last word — do you think the Mistress knows?

EURYCLEIA: Of course she knows. The legend of Ulysses reached here long before he did. But hush up now! That's their private domain.

(Pause)

PHILOETIUS: What's he doing right now?

EUMAEUS: He's in his bath. He's steeping and sighing with pleasure in water that's finally clean. I had to scrape him off. I had to change the water. I changed it five times.

EURYCLEIA: Five times! Did you have enough hot water?

EUMAEUS: No, of course not. For half an hour, two of my swineherds that I'd brought to help me ran back and forth from the bathroom to the kitchen. Boy, did they gallop! You should have seen them. All this time I was scrubbing. And you better believe I scrubbed hard. But the dirt had got so far down under the skin that it was like a tattoo. I'm telling you, for awhile I thought those guys in the Trojan War tattooed their hide! *(The others laugh.)* But it really was dirt. I finally got it out.

PHILOETIUS: So, is he happy?

EUMAEUS: Delighted! Before I left, I told my two helpers not to let him go to sleep. They'll get him out of the water and then they'll massage him and rub him with oil. All groomed and rejuvenated, you won't even recognize him. *(To Philoetius)* Oh, I forgot, he said for us to make sure the big hall downstairs had been scoured and hosed down to get rid of the smell of blood.

PHILOETIUS: I saw to that, it's already done. A nasty job, too. We had to scoop the blood up off the floor with shovels. The slaughterhouse smell was enough to make you sick. Now we'll have to burn sulphur in there and air it out for at least a couple of days. You want to go get started?

EUMAEUS: Yes, might as well. *(To Eurycleia)* What's the Mistress doing?

EURYCLEIA: Why, she . . . she's getting ready.

PHILOETIUS: For what?

(Everyone laughs discreetly.)

The fact is, she probably doesn't remember too well how to do it.

SECOND MAIDSERVANT: *(Seriously)* Oh, yes she does, don't worry. Love is something you don't forget how to do.

PHILOETIUS: *(Laughing)* How do you know?

SECOND MAIDSERVANT: I can feel it. *(Ardently)* Once you've known it, you have it inside you.

EUMAEUS: I'll take your word for it, but still, twenty years!

FIRST MAIDSERVANT: *(Dreamily)* Yes, twenty years. Twenty times one year of . . . chastity. Especially since Master, before he left for the war, obviously had great . . . requirements.

SECOND MAIDSERVANT: *(Very sincere)* I know I could never do it.

(Everyone laughs again, still subdued.)

FIRST MAIDSERVANT: Unless . . . unless Mistress managed to . . . how should I say . . . console herself a little?

EURYCLEIA: *(Sternly)* Think what you're saying!

FIRST MAIDSERVANT: *(Very quickly)* Oh, I only meant one time, here and there. With all these men around her, urging her to give in, it must not have been very easy to resist.

EURYCLEIA: *(Severely)* Silence! Now that this household is back to normal, thank the gods, try to get it into your head that the Mistress has another idea of what's easy than you do.

EUMAEUS: The Master too. Both of them have gone through harder things in life than working out a reunion night. *(Pause)* Well! I think we've said about everything. *(To Philoetius)* Do you know where the sulphur is?

PHILOETIUS: In the saddle-room, on the highest shelf of the little cupboard in the back. Telemachus told me in the middle of a yawn big enough to split his jaws.

EUMAEUS: Where is he now?

PHILOETIUS: He's in bed, poor kid. He won't wake up tonight, you can be sure of that.

EUMAEUS: That battle of brutes was hard on a young man barely out of adolescence.

PHILOETIUS: I went up to see him before I came in here. I never saw anybody so sacked out.

[***]

EURYCLEIA: Well, let him sleep, the dear boy and after awhile, when he wakes up . . . *(She stops to listen.)* Hear that? Someone's coming *(Pointing to the door at stage left)*, that way. *(Pause)*

EUMAEUS: *(In a stage whisper)* The Mistress, you think?

EURYCLEIA: *(Also in a stage whisper)* Who else would it be? Is the bed made?

FIRST MAIDSERVANT: Yes, and well made.

SECOND MAIDSERVANT: If you want to go look . . .

EURYCLEIA: No, it's too late. I hope

for your sake that you know your job. If you don't . . . *(She stops short.)* Here she comes! *(Everyone stands up and remains at attention. The left door opens. Penelope comes in, dressed for bed, with a hooded white cloak over her nightgown. Everyone bows.)* Good evening, Mistress.

PENELOPE: Good evening.

EURYCLEIA: *(Anxiously)* The Mistress is very pale. *(She goes over to her.)* Are you ill, Mistress?

PENELOPE: *(Distracted)* Yes . . . no . . . I'm not sure. *(Pause. She sits down, breathes deeply and then says in a more assured voice.)* I would like to know who . . . assassinated those girls, outside? *(Bombshell. Everyone looks at the floor. Pause. Penelope persists.)* Those girls, right out there in front of the stables? When I was closing my window for the night, I leaned out and . . . God! What a sight! Hanged! A dozen of them, yes, hanged! Who? Who did that?

EURYCLEIA: *(Reluctantly)* They weren't girls anymore, Mistress, they were women.

EUMAEUS: Bad women, cowardly, false. They'd been rotten for years.

PENELOPE: Are you sure? These things happen quickly, you know.

PHILOETIUS: If the Mistress will pardon me, I don't mind saying that I've come on them several times in my night rounds . . .

PENELOPE: *(Interrupting him)* One moment, please. *(To the two maidservants)* Girls, tell me, have you finished what you had to do in this room?

FIRST MAIDSERVANT: Yes, Mistress.

***Translator's note: I have omitted a three-line comment by Eumaeus here because I am convinced the expression on which the comment is based is untranslatable. Eumaeus says, "Télémaque en écrase," meaning that Telemachus is exhausted and sleeping soundly. The "en" refers to "punaises" (bedbugs), which Telemachus is "crushing" in his sound sleep. The suggestion is not that the beds in Ulysses' house are infested; Eumaeus uses the expression as a novelty, to emphasize how heavily Telemachus flopped onto his bed after the massacre of the suitors.*

SECOND MAIDSERVANT: It was the bed. It's made.

PENELOPE: Nothing is detaining you then from going back to your rooms?

FIRST MAIDSERVANT: No, Mistress.

SECOND MAIDSERVANT: Nothing at all.

PENELOPE: Then you may go. And sleep well. *(The two girls curtsy.)* I imagine that everyone in this house, after such a trying day, needs sleep. A good, long sleep.

THE TWO MAIDSERVANTS: Good night, Mistress.

PENELOPE: Good night. *(The girls leave. Penelope turns to Philoetius.)* All right, Philoetius, now. What were you going to say?

PHILOETIUS: Well, that five or six times, at night when I was making my rounds, I came on one or the other of those girls sneaking out of the room of one of those men that are still smoldering in the back courtyard — or sneaking in, depending on the time. I ought to tell you that when I make my rounds I always take off my boots and wear sandals, so I don't make any noise walking. You can't imagine all the things I came on some nights last summer! When I think that from the outside the house seemed calm, like everybody was sleeping . . . I've always hesitated to tell the Mistress . . .

PENELOPE: You should have told me.

PHILOETIUS: I know, but the Mistress already had enough troubles managing this huge estate alone. We talked about it, Eumaeus and Eurycleia and me . . .

EUMAEUS: Oh, yes, we talked about it. But we didn't know exactly what to do.

EURYCLEIA: These young people, you know, even the best ones, they're very outspoken and they do just what they please.

(Pause)

PENELOPE: *(Slowly)* I understand. Yes, I understand all that, but tell me honestly: do you think they deserved to be killed?

EUMAEUS: *(Quickly)* They weren't killed, Mistress, they were executed. There's a difference.

PHILOETIUS: Oh, yeah, a big difference.

PENELOPE: Executed, the poor things! Who did that!

EUMAEUS: God forgive me, I think it was . . . *(Quickly)* It was Telemachus.

PENELOPE: *(With a start)* Telemachus, my god! *(Stunned)* But never . . . no, never . . . *(She breaks off, overwhelmed.)*

EUMAEUS: *(Gently)* If there's one thing, Mistress, that your son has refused to pardon since he's been old enough to think like a man, it's that somebody act with disrespect to you, his mother and the wife of Ulysses — anybody, whoever it might be, servant or prince, slave or king. And those girls, ten times a day, one or the other of them, spoke inconsiderately of you, and little by little, as time passed and the return of Ulysses became more improbable, they spoke with complete freedom.

EURYCLEIA: At first, Telemachus didn't pay any attention. He was just a nice little boy that the serving girls played with like a big doll. But all of a sudden . . . I can see that day so clearly . . .

PHILOETIUS: So can I.

EUMAEUS: Me too. It was an evening in April, mild, the fields turning green . . .

PHILOETIUS: Yes, toward the end of April.

EUMAEUS: We were all three talking about the household. All of a sudden . . .

EURYCLEIA: Yes, suddenly Telemachus came in. How old would he have been then? Fourteen?

PHILOETIUS: Yes, fourteen or fifteen. I can just see him: he was pale and his whole body was trembling, I swear it! He was shaking the way you shake when it's freezing cold.

EURYCLEIA: We had to drag the story out of him a bit at a time, with incredible effort, because at fifteen a child is so ill-prepared to maneuver in a world of deceit and schemes, it's as foreign to him, as unbreathable as the bottom of the sea is to men. One of the girls had boasted that she knew why your interminable tapestry was . . . interminable, that's the word. Some of the girls of course, seeing her take off on this dangerous claim, had tried to get her to be quiet, but two or three others encouraged her and she started shouting bitter sarcastic remarks about how the Mistress was a hypocrite, and she threatened to give the secret away to her lover, the suitor Euryades, as soon as she went to his room that night.

EUMAEUS: So poor Telemachus learned in one fell swoop that there were serving girls in the house who hated their masters and that these famous suitors, who seemed to have no more pressing worry than to court his mother, were really nothing but libertines who were not above sharing their beds with a servant. A rude awakening, you must admit, and it happened so fast, for a child not even fifteen years old.

EURYCLEIA: I can still see him, crying with rage and helplessness . . . Naturally we dried his tears and stayed by his bed to talk to him quietly until he went to sleep. The next day, when he woke up, nothing remained with him from the previous evening's scene, or that's what you would have thought, but we knew him and we were sure he wouldn't forget, and that one fine day, when the right chance came, that insolent girl and her presumptuous lover would be punished without pity.

PHILOETIUS: Which is what happened today: Euryades was finished off with an expert javelin shot, by Telemachus, in the banquet hall, and the girl was hanged, with eleven like her, in front of the stables, also by Telemachus. And I'm sure that when he did it, the child of fifteen, now a young man of twenty-two, remembered that he had sworn one day to punish, in one blow, the presumption of one and the insolence of the other.

(Pause)

EUMAEUS: All I saw was Euryades finished off . . .

PHILOETIUS: *(Laughing gloomily)* . . . along with a few others!

EUMAEUS: *(Also laughing gloomily)* Along with a few others. I couldn't watch the punishment of the women.

EURYCLEIA: I didn't see anything.

PHILOETIUS: Oh, it was simple. The

prince took a ship's cable and strung it along the top of the columns around the porch, so that their feet couldn't touch the ground. So, with their heads all in a line and a rope around their necks, the girls suffered the most atrocious death. Their feet jerked for a minute, but not for long.

EURYCLEIA: *(Echoing Philoetius)* The most atrocious death . . . *(She shivers.)*

EUMAEUS: *(Eagerly)* Hey, hold on there! You can't judge a punishment, even a hideous one, when your head is cool and your heart is at rest. You have to get inside the skin of the man that inflicted it, as much as you can, you have to imagine how it was to strike out in the furor of battle, to feel your heart pounding in your chest the way his was, to feel your head spinning with fever and images of blood. Because one thing is certain: at moments like that, nobody is his own master. Telemachus wasn't himself, Ulysses wasn't either. He had just ordered the execution of the girls . . .

PENELOPE: Ah! It was Ulysses who . . .

EUMAEUS: Yes, Mistress. Telemachus would never have taken it on himself. Ulysses was rushing the whole matter. "When you've put the hall back in order," he shouted, "bring out the serving girls and take their lives at swordpoint, and don't spare a single one! The call of Aphrodite and nightly pleasures in the suitors' beds are over."

PHILOETIUS: Yes, that's what he shouted. I heard him while Eumaeus and Telemachus and me were scraping the ground with shovels to get the blood up. I

remember the smell was nauseating . . .

EUMAEUS: You already said it was: the slaughterhouse smell was enough to make you sick. All right. But now that the hall is probably dried out after the women washed it, we can spread the sulphur around and air it out for awhile.

PHILOETIUS: By God, you're right, we still have that to do. I'd forgotten. *(To Eumaeus)* Let's go, buddy.

PENELOPE: Just a minute longer, please. How did the death of the serving girls pass from Ulysses to Telemachus? I would like to see it clearly.

PHILOETIUS: You want to tell the Mistress, Eumaeus?

EUMAEUS: Wait, I'm trying to remember. Things happened so fast. Let's see . . . I can still hear the screams of the serving girls while they were working.

PHILOETIUS: Hideous cries! Because they knew they were condemned, Ulysses had made no secret of their fate — condemned, yes, but serving girls to the end. And that's what they were. I can see them wringing out the sponges to scrub the tables and chairs. They were crying so hard they seemed to be washing the furniture with their tears. Then they took out the bodies of the dead suitors. Ah, all those girls, already practically dead themselves, wracked with sobs, carrying out dead men on their backs.

EUMAEUS: Some of them were too heavy. So two of the girls would get together and drag him out. And they screamed, they bellowed in despair. Yes, all those women!

14

PHILOETIUS: And that little brunette that suddenly fainted and was hanged, I think, without regaining consciousness.

PENELOPE: *(As if to herself)* This is appalling!

EUMAEUS: "Hurry up! Hurry up!" Ulysses was shouting, "You're going beyond the time of your existence," until finally everything was back in order in the hall, the girls were taken out and herded together in a corner of the courtyard, between the pavilion and the outside wall, and then Telemachus came forward: "It will not be said," he shouted, "that an honorable death ended the vile lives of these women who brought disgrace to my mother and to me. No sword for them, but the rope!" "Excellent," shouted Ulysses. And then Telemachus took the ship's cable . . .

(Long silence. Penelope, overcome, has let her head fall into her hands.)

EUMAEUS: *(Quietly)* Mistress, I was repelled by the execution of the serving girls too. You can't watch in cold blood while twelve creatures, young ones, are strangled, painfully. And anyway, I didn't see anything. I turned toward the wall, and then I left with my eyes on the ground. I'll leave you to imagine what the screaming of the girls was like. But when I got to the house, the screams stopped short . . . and I knew the cord had gone taut and silenced them.

(Silence again, longer this time. Eumaeus continues in the same tone of voice.) Still you can't forget that they claimed the Mistress was a hypocrite.

PHILOETIUS: *(Quietly)* Or that they

acted as if the Mistress really had been a hypocrite, and of the worst kind.

EURYCLEIA: *(Quietly)* Or that afterward they ran to the suitors and told them the secret of the tapestry. Which caused any number of problems for us, the most serious of which was that the Mistress was obliged to complete her work . . .

EUMAEUS: And everything that followed from that.

(Pause. Penelope appears numb, her head still hidden between her hands. Seeing this, Eumaeus and Philoetius agree by signals to go about their job of spreading sulphur in the banquet hall; they tiptoe out. Eurycleia remains alone with Penelope. Silence)

PENELOPE: *(Slowly)* When you really think about it, tell me — what else was I, hm? What else was I but a hypocrite?

EURYCLEIA: Mistress!

PENELOPE: I thought I was very clever, but who asked me to play games with those young men, to invent the story of my woman's work I had to finish before I could do anything else? No, really, the whole thing is childish. All I had to do was tell the truth, all I had to do, once and for all, was tell the truth.

EURYCLEIA: But, Mistress, you told it! You were forced to spell it out to everybody after those bitches had gone sneaking off to the suitors and told them what was going on. And for what, hm? What good did it do? The tapestry, which hadn't budged for years from the red rose in the lower right corner, suddenly started growing by giant steps across the whole right side, then over to the other side, toward the white rose in the upper left corner. And you were obliged to complete it. Just think, in another two or three days, if Ulysses hadn't come back, we would have been forced to choose somebody out of that crowd of young fools and take him for a husband. That's what you had promised, Mistress, and Penelope has only one word . . .

PENELOPE: (Very quietly) Yes . . . Yes, yes. (She begins to cry noiselessly.)

EURYCLEIA: (Alarmed) What is it, Mistress? (She goes over to Penelope.) Tell me, Mistress, what is it?

PENELOPE: (Anguished) Oh, Nurse, I don't know, I really don't know.

(Pause)

EURYCLEIA: (Gently) Well, I do. The day of the reunion has come, and it's not the way we imagined it. But what of it? Do I need to tell you that reality never reproduces the beauty and richness of dreams? You can believe an old woman who all through her life has never known a dream that wasn't disappointing. So here we are. Such as it is, today is a gift of the gods, a priceless gift because you came so close to not receiving it at all. Ulysses could have been shipwrecked in view of Ithaca, or lost at sea, without finding the island. The suitors could have defeated him or wounded him fatally. You yourself could have been remarried, Mistress. And a thousand other things could have happened . . .

PENELOPE: But, Nurse, you don't realize. Between what I was expecting and what happened, at certain moments a chasm opens up, a chasm so frightful . . .

(A knock at the door, stage right. Penelope starts, straightens up quickly, and wipes her eyes. Another knock)

PENELOPE: (Her voice unsure) Yes. Come in.

(Ulysses enters. He too is in night clothes, dark blue pajamas and a light-colored bathrobe.)

ULYSSES: (Cheerfully) I don't know if I've put on weight or if, in twenty years, this material has shrunk. Look at it! (He stands in such a way, with his back hunched and his arms stretched out, that the clothes don't seem to fit him.) What do you think, darling?

PENELOPE: (Without enthusiasm) If you want me to see what's the matter, you'll have to take off your robe. (She holds out her arm, and Ulysses grabs it playfully and kisses her hand.)

ULYSSES: (Laughing) No, no, darling, my dearest wife. It was just a joke, an innocent joke, the kind you make when you're getting ready for bed, when you're very tired, but you still feel like laughing. Look how well my clothes fit me!

PENELOPE: (Seriously) Excuse me.

ULYSSES: Of course! Of course I excuse you. In twenty years of separation, you've forgotten my penchant for jokes — a penchant which the old blind poet (who could see very well) honored with a series of epithets that can only be described as . . . Homeric—the wily Ulysses, the man of a thousand tricks, the man as cunning as a monkey. This penchant never left me, you see, not even at the worst moments.

PENELOPE: *(Still serious)* Excuse me!

ULYSSES: *(Smiling)* Again? *(He goes over to a chair.)* I think it was . . . *(He sits down.)* Yes, I'm sure it was a sort of defense against old age, that I felt coming closer to me every day. A way of prolonging the carefree years and the smile of my youth, against all odds. *(He stretches.)* Ah! This is great! *(Silently, Eurycleia rushes to slip a cushion under his feet.)* Thank you, Nurse. At least you haven't grown old. Still as attentive as ever. *(He straightens up in the chair.)* By Zeus, you can't imagine how great I feel! If you knew how many times I've imagined the moment I'm living right now — my house, finally free . . . my wife, our room. *(Silence. Ulysses thinks and then says in an entirely different voice, strangely assertive.)* I'm 49 years old. Do you know that?

EURYCLEIA: *(After a slight pause)* The prime of life!

ULYSSES: *(Ironically)* Oh, come now! When I say 49, it's because I still want to linger on the side of the 40's. But in fact . . .

EURYCLEIA: What's got into you? Everybody knows, and I better than anybody, that you were born at the end of December. Since it's only the middle of September now, you're still in your forties. And you will be for three more months, plenty of time for a new life.

(Pause)

ULYSSES: Forty-nine years old! *(He shakes his head.)* What else can one inspire, at that age, what feeling can one arouse — shall we say in the fair sex —

besides respect, obedience, respectful obedience . . . which the young pretend to feel, in order to be left alone and escape from these gray hairs and this face lined with wrinkles?

PENELOPE: *(Smiling, but without tenderness)* You'll have a hard time convincing me that Nausicaa, for instance, showed nothing but obedience to you *(She laughs.)* and respect!

ULYSSES: *(Like a young man)* Nausicaa! Ah! What a happy surprise to hear that enchanting name from your beautiful lips! But I didn't know you knew the story. Who told you?

PENELOPE: I know everything about you, you may as well get used to it. The "old blind poet" spared me no detail.

ULYSSES: *(Smiling)* If you know "everything," you are not unaware of the reality behind certain . . . appearances. *(Changing his approach)* Yes, it's true that Alcinous, the king, would not have minded having me marry his daughter. Nor would his daughter, Nausicaa, have minded it either. But both of them found out very quickly how things stood with me: that I was married, and that I was king of my island, and that nothing was dearer to me than my island and my wife. So, the evening of the first day, Alcinous had a ship fitted out . . .

PENELOPE: *(Interrupting him)* I know! Oh, I'm quite aware that the man of a thousand tricks has no trouble recounting all his actions, the good ones and the less good ones, in a favorable light.

ULYSSES: *(Continuing as if nothing had been said)* . . . fitted out a ship, as I said, with a crew of experienced sailors, to bring me back home. Did you hear? The evening of the first day. Now that that's settled, I'm willing to admit the episode in Phaeacia turned out to be enjoyable. It was restful, congenial, and my memory of it is very . . . pleasant.

PENELOPE: *(Bitterly)* And what was I doing here, all alone, during this . . . pleasantness? Hm? What was I doing but unraveling a tapestry every night so I could weave it again the next day? And do you know why I was unraveling that tapestry?

ULYSSES: Yes, but . . . I don't remember who told me. I thought the trick of the tapestry was very . . . endearing, and ingenious, worthy of Ulysses' wife.

PENELOPE: *(Still bitter)* Endearing? Ha! Endearing, really?

ULYSSES: Yes, really. Why are you . . . am I rubbing you the wrong way? *(Silence. Penelope looks down and remains obstinately quiet. Ulysses gets up and walks around the room, distracted. Pause)*

EURYCLEIA: *(Carefully)* Well! I'm going to say good night, children, and go to bed. I advise you to do the same. The day has been long and tiring. Since things are finally quiet, we should take advantage of it. So! Good night!

PENELOPE: Good night, Nurse.

ULYSSES: Sleep well, old friend.

(Eurycleia goes out. Long pause)

PENELOPE: One question, Ulysses.

ULYSSES: *(Distracted)* Ask anything you want.

PENELOPE: When you returned, did you find things in order, in good condition, I mean everything you inspected: the house, the land, the treasure — all our possessions?

ULYSSES: I found everything perfect. It was the way I left it, except better. In fact, much better, clearly improved.

PENELOPE: I'm glad to hear you say so.

ULYSSES: I say it with pleasure.

PENELOPE: Good. Now, do you think that all this progress, these improvements, accomplished during your absence, or not even the improvements, just the maintenance alone, keeping things in the condition they were in when you left, do you think that all this took place spontaneously, without effort, without worry?

ULYSSES: That's the farthest thing from my mind! I know very well it was you, and you alone, whose constant attention is responsible for the excellent condition of our property and the increase in our holdings. To which *(He laughs.)*, my dear, we will soon add what I brought back from my travels and left hidden yesterday in a cave. It's not bad, you'll see!

PENELOPE: One thing at a time!

ULYSSES: Agreed. I just wanted you to know . . .

PENELOPE: *(Interrupting him)* All right, in a minute. And how do you think a young woman eighteen years old, your young wife — because I was eighteen when you left, Ulysses — how do you think this young woman, inept, through her youth and inexperience, at everything except loving you, how do you think she managed to face a mass of obligations, of material necessities: expenses, collections, leases and rentals, contracts, debts, claims, a whole world of duties of which I understood not a shred and which I had to begin understanding fast, I assure you, or else watch the holdings of the house of Ulysses melt, in a few moments, like snow in the sun. So, tell me, with you gone, have I been a good replacement? A good overseer of the estate?

ULYSSES: *(Warmly)* A good one? What are you talking about? Penelope, you were a very good, a superb . . . you proved yourself a peerless overseer of the house of Ulysses, that's obvious! And I don't mind admitting . . .

PENELOPE: Let me finish. This good overseer, worthy, I imagine, of a reward, or at least of consideration . . .

ULYSSES: Worthy of consideration, you say! Of every consideration. And I have every intention . . .

PENELOPE: *(Smiling)* Dear eternal storyteller! I know you're eager to launch into that subject, but for the moment I have the floor — let me finish. This good, this superb overseer of your property, how did you greet her today? What was your first gesture upon your homecoming? *(Pause)* You greeted her with murder, with a massacre, and in the house whose keys she was intending to return to you so you could admire the cleanliness, the luxury, the embellishments — with the extermination of over a hundred men. Somewhat crude men, it's true, unrefined, I agree, some of them even brutish, but who after all aspired to nothing worse than taking me for a wife, which did honor to your choice and was

rather flattering. And I'm not even counting the savage execution of a dozen of my serving girls. As a homecoming gesture, you must admit it was spectacular.

ULYSSES: *(Dumfounded)* What is she saying? Hm? What has she just said? Now, my dear, let's get this straight right now, let's get it perfectly straight. Otherwise I'm wasting my breath. *(Slowly)* Are you by chance criticizing me for putting the suitors to death?

PENELOPE: Exactly.

ULYSSES: All right. Very good, I'm willing to understand . . . anything. So, in your opinion, if I follow what you're saying, I should have been satisfied with . . . with what, exactly? Throwing them out? Fine. Now just imagine how that would work. Let's say I drive them to the door by kicking them, for example. (A hundred kicks! Feature that!) Then I throw them out into the street and swear at them. And the deed is done?

PENELOPE: Not in the least! Not in the least! I don't see why you would have felt the need to be more crude than they were. The "deed" would have required neither kicking nor swearing. All you had to do was ask them to leave. With you back home, they had no more reason to stay. And they would have understood that.

ULYSSES: You think they would.

PENELOPE: I know they would. Eurymachus, for instance—you know the one I'm talking about?

ULYSSES: Yes, I know the one. He's one of the leaders of the local young men, isn't he?

PENELOPE: That's right. And what did Eurymachus do as soon as he recognized you, as soon as he knew beyond any doubt that it was really Ulysses he was hearing? Hm? Well, I'll tell you. He spoke to you. He established contact.

ULYSSES: But . . .

PENELOPE: Don't contradict me, I know he did. From my room I can hear everything that goes on in the hall. I didn't understand all the words, but I followed the tone of his comments very well. Besides, one of your friends confirmed what I heard. Eurymachus spoke with you. Calmly and reasonably. "If it's you," he said, "if it's really Ulysses standing before me — and I don't doubt it anymore — you're entirely justified in reproaching us for all the excesses we've indulged in on your property. But I swear to you that all that is over now. Let us make peace with you. We'll find the means to reimburse you for everything we drank and ate in your house. What would you think, for instance, of some heavy fine, say twenty head of cattle from each of us? Just imagine the herd your drovers would have to take care of — a hundred times twenty head of cattle! Not bad, eh?" (Pause) There was a silence, and naïve as I was, I supposed you were reflecting on the offer, you were wondering if twenty head was enough. But, as you know, that was hardly the case! Suddenly I heard your voice, choking with rage, lurching out of your throat: "Twenty head of cattle!" you shouted, "twenty head! What a laugh! To reimburse me? You could bring me every shred of your property, and the property of

your families, and of everybody else on the island, I would still hunt you down until I had complete revenge!" After that announcement, you began striking out in rage, like a madman. And the first to fall, struck square in the chest, I found out, was poor Eurymachus.

(Pause. Ulysses repeats quietly.)

ULYSSES: Poor Eurymachus. (Pause. Then he continues, louder, more assured.) Never, do you hear me, never in all the scenes I've dreamed up, the reconstructions of you I've gone through, during the past ten years, when I imagined us together again, you and I, as we are right now, or at the table for a meal, or even in our marriage bed, when I invented the words we would say to each other to test our reunion, to prove ourselves, never did I imagine on your tongue the name of an adversary, an enemy of Ulysses, pronounced with this . . . indulgence, this charm, this gentleness, yes, almost tenderly. (He repeats.) "Poor Eurymachus . . ."

PENELOPE: (Shrugging her shoulders) Tenderly!

ULYSSES: (Angrily) Tenderly! Certainly, my dear, I realized that in my absence you'd change, but not like this! (In a quieter voice) Not like this!

(Pause)

PENELOPE: I'm twenty years older, that's all. My view of men and the world has broadened and become more assured. But nothing in me, nothing essential has happened to transform the young girl that you took for a wife, Ulysses. I still have that young girl's heart which regrets . . . *(Changing moods)* Yes, it's true, I regret . . . I regret deeply that you have killed a man who had hardly offended you and who was making a generous offer to repair all the damage inflicted on our house. I will ever admit to you that I will try not to think too much about this . . . episode with Eurymachus, or I would hold it against you always.

ULYSSES: *(Very assertively)* What am I hearing? "He had hardly offended me"? Really? Do you have any idea of the life I was leading, while this . . . Eurymachus was "not offending me"?

PENELOPE: I didn't say that. I didn't say "not at all."

ULYSSES: Watched, tracked, pursued relentlessly from one end to the other of an interminable sea, without really knowing why. The old blind poet claims I had offended the gods, but . . . do you think there are enough gods left in the skies to offend? Constantly at sea. Condemned to remain, to live at sea! Without relief, do you understand that? Without relief, dancing on the sea, like the sea! Always walking on the deck of a dancing ship, dancing day and night, forced to match my earth creature's step to the whim of this dancing ship. Can you imagine that? Can you imagine how I walked? How I had to walk? Watch: one long step, slow, gliding to keep your balance against the heave, like a fencer's ploy. Come over here with me, I'll show you . . .

PENELOPE: No, thanks, I can imagine it.

ULYSSES: . . . then two or three short,

galloping steps to catch up with the rhythm *(He does the steps.)*, then a long step again, a giant step and you crash into the gunwale—when your ship has a gunwale. Can you imagine that? Hm? Can you see a man, a man like me, forced to live at that pace? Forced to make his decisions — and what decisions can you make in such an indecisive life? — while adapting, while accommodating his gait to the pitch and roll of the ship, with never a chance for this gait to approximate human form! And at night, the same story—impossible to sleep comfortably. Always this movement, like a swing *(He imitates.)*, up and down, and up and down, always! And with no break or relief or recreation of any kind!

PENELOPE: What do you mean, with no break? Don't forget that I know everything about your life and that I am aware of the . . . recreation you offered yourself. It's true that my information is lacking in details, but I expect you can fill them in. Tell me, for instance, before we go any further, who was . . . let's see . . . Circe? That marvelous Circe—oh, an extraordinary woman—who occupies a significant place in your adventure.

ULYSSES: *(Laughing bitterly)* Circe! Ha! You made a bad choice. One of the worst memories from my travels. A witch, that's all, nothing but a woman who . . .

PENELOPE: *(Cutting him off)* Young and pretty, naturally.

ULYSSES: How could one say of a woman who participates in the world of magic and who therefore changes skin and appearance twenty or thirty times a day, how could one say that she *is* young and pretty?

PENELOPE: What are you talking about? This Circe really changed her skin?

ULYSSES: No! That's a manner of speaking. She changed—imperceptibly, I agree, but I swear you could see it—she changed shape and . . . appearance and . . . style, that's the right word, and therefore age and personality, at least twenty times a day according to which mirror she was reflected in along the walls of her house.

PENELOPE: A beautiful house?

ULYSSES: Oh, a splendid house.

PENELOPE: Prettier than mine?

ULYSSES: Not at all the same kind. I came upon her two or three times, making faces in the big mirror in the hall . . .

PENELOPE: What were you doing in the hall?

ULYSSES: I don't have the faintest recollection, I was . . . passing by, I suppose.

PENELOPE: You were passing by—just like that? Going from where to where?

ULYSSES: (*Impatiently*) Oh! Don't get technical! Don't make my task of remembering insurmountable! (*Bruskly*) I was in the corridor, one of the numerous corridors of the house . . .

PENELOPE: Ground floor or upstairs?

ULYSSES: Ground floor.

PENELOPE: You're sure?

ULYSSES: (*Irritated*) Yes. Perfectly. If you make me tell about my travels at this rate, we'll be at it for ten years!

PENELOPE: I don't trust you. You're a storyteller. You always take the long way around. Not out of malice, or with the intention of deceiving, but by nature, because you were born a storyteller, a seeker of effects and digressions, because it delights you to lead people on to think what you want them to think. But I, my dear, am the opposite of a storyteller. I cut things short, I go straight to the heart of the matter, not with the intention of finding fault with you, but to discover the truth, if occasionally it is in your power to tell the truth. Do you understand?

ULYSSES: (*With ill-concealed annoyance*) You're not very subtle. So, I was telling you that I came upon her . . .

PENELOPE: Came upon whom?

ULYSSES: Circe, of course. Aren't we talking about Circe?

PENELOPE: Among other women, yes.

ULYSSES: Well, so I came upon her two or three times making faces in the mirror. Sometimes she was delighted and smiled at her image. Sometimes she was sullen, haughty, angrily correcting some feature, some expression she didn't like. With Circe, believe me, you went in less than five minutes from the charming face of a young girl, bright, sharp, a little unsettling, to a serene face, slightly heavy, but full of assurance, the satisfied assurance of a woman spoiled by life. But at any rate, she never kept the same appearance for more than a quarter of an hour.

PENELOPE: Well, bravo! This woman had what it takes to seduce an expert like you. Twenty women in one, that's a dream come true.

ULYSSES: Stop using that mocking tone

of voice. It doesn't suit you.

PENELOPE: Very well! What tone shall I use?

ULYSSES: Your own, my dear wife, your own, the voice that followed me, accompanied me on my wanderings. Because it's strange I never lost the memory of your voice. It stayed faithfully stored away in my ears. Your voice, your laugh, your turns of phrase. But your features, for example, left me. Almost immediately. You can't imagine the trouble I had to go to to bring them back to mind. Naturally I *knew* you had a beautiful face, clear and candid, your own face, but I couldn't *see* it, I lost sight of it. All that remained in my mind's eye was a black speck, surrounded by shining rays, what remains in your eye after you've looked at the sun face to face and you're dazzled.

PENELOPE: Tell me, did Circe's face escape you the way mine did?

ULYSSES: Not at all. I remember it in every detail. If I were a painter, I could draw it for you right now.

PENELOPE: That of course means there is a basic difference between her and me.

ULYSSES: *(Exuberantly)* A difference! My dear, the difference from you to her is so great, so enormous, that when I say her charm and your beauty, I'm not even talking about the same feminine attribute. You're so peaceful, so calm and smiling, that I'd even say . . .

PENELOPE: All right, hold on!

ULYSSES: What?

PENELOPE: I don't trust your storytelling.

ULYSSES: What storytelling? Aren't you calm and smiling?

PENELOPE: *(Smiling)* Yes, I am. But don't be misled. Tell me now: Circe's house, that "splendid" house, did you go through it?

ULYSSES: Mmm . . . I don't remember.

PENELOPE: Come now, you know perfectly well if that woman took you on a tour of the premises.

ULYSSES: No, I don't remember. I remember a vestibule, a long corridor . . .

PENELOPE: The one with the mirrors?

ULYSSES: Exactly. And a staircase of marble, I think. *(He concentrates, then says without hesitation.)* Yes, it was marble, I'm sure of it. And then a huge room where I waited for the return of my crew, after they had become men again.

PENELOPE: Is it true that she had changed them into animals? Into pigs, I was told?

ULYSSES: Pigs, yes, that's right.

PENELOPE: Strange idea! Strange woman! In other words, a competitor for Eumaeus.

ULYSSES: Yes, that's about it. *(He laughs.)* But she didn't take care of her animals the way Eumaeus does. A little water, a crust of bread, and that was all she thought they deserved. I often wondered . . .

PENELOPE: *(Interrupting him)* I too have wondered. But one thing at a time. So, you were saying, a huge room — a reception room, is that right?

ULYSSES: Yes, that's right. That's about all I remember.

PENELOPE: I see. *(Abruptly)* What about the bedroom?

ULYSSES: Ah! The . . . bedroom?

PENELOPE: Yes, the bedroom. Did you see it?

ULYSSES: I . . . don't quite remember.

PENELOPE: Of course you remember. Come on, storyteller, tell your story. What was the bed like?

ULYSSES: The . . . bed?

PENELOPE: Yes, the bed.

ULYSSES: It's hazy. As far as I can recall, it was a monumental thing. A monument in bronze and gold, with purple sheets spread over lawn on the bottom layer.

PENELOPE: See how well you remember! You've given a remarkable description of the bed. Did you get up on it?

ULYSSES: On what?

PENELOPE: On the bed. Don't tell me that this detail has deserted your memory. One always remembers climbing to the top of a monument. (Pause) Well?

ULYSSES: I think — notice that I say I think —because the whole episode was so long ago; I may have stretched out on it for a few minutes.

PENELOPE: And she did too?

ULYSSES: Naturally she did too. That's why I got up there.

PENELOPE: How did you get up there?

ULYSSES: What do you mean, how did I get up there?

PENELOPE: I mean, how does one make such a maneuver? You'll have to forgive me, but I do not have the same experience you do of the various beds, couches, and divans of the Mediterranean world.

ULYSSES: I got up there by taking hold of the straps, which I managed without difficulty. (Taking a different tack) You have to

see things the way they were. This woman was very proud of . . . of her possessions: her house, her garden, her furniture, her jewels. I saw what she wanted. She wanted people to go into ecstasies. So I went into ecstasies, it's as simple as that.

PENELOPE: In the bed? In her company? Did she go into ecstasies too?

ULYSSES: (Very annoyed) Oh! (Regaining control) I tried out the bed, the softness of the bed, by bouncing on it two or three times. I said something like, "Yes, indeed, a fine bed you have here!" She lapped it up. I took advantage of her satisfaction and worked myself into her good graces. We laughed, and then I asked her, as if it were a joke, to promise me whatever I wanted, with the gods as witness.

PENELOPE: She consented to that?

ULYSSES: She didn't bat an eyelash.

PENELOPE: Without knowing what she was committing herself to! What a fool!

ULYSSES: I didn't show my hand until she had already sworn her oath. Then I asked her to free my men. She said all right immediately, with no hedging.

PENELOPE: If I had been in her place, you wouldn't have had me like that.

ULYSSES: I'm sure I would not. But you, my dear, are unique. I have never met your equal in the world.

PENELOPE: (Flattered) Oh, is that so?

ULYSSES: I assure you that you will occupy a place among the immortals. Only one goddess, a single one, Athena, could perhaps give you advice on the matter of precautions, guarantees, assurances, and other safety measures to be observed before entering into one of these contracts people seem to make — none of which I understand in the least.

PENELOPE: (Impetuously) All right, but swear to me right now, no more discussion, swear to me that you didn't do anything with her in that bed.

ULYSSES: (Immediately) I swear it! Except, of course, the agreement I got her to make. (He repeats.) I swear it!

PENELOPE: Better than that! Hold out your arm. Open your right hand!

ULYSSES: (Complying) I swear it!

PENELOPE: Careful! Think about it!

ULYSSES: No, I don't need to. I swear it and I'll prove it. While I was talking in the bed with Circe, the servants were all around us tending to the manor. You must admit, it would have taken real shrewdness to . . . let's use the word, make love to Circe in front of witnesses.

PENELOPE: Exactly what you do not lack!

ULYSSES: What?

PENELOPE: Shrewdness.

ULYSSES: (Delighted) Oh! You remember?

PENELOPE: (Dryly) Yes. So, these girls, the servants, what were they doing in the manor?

ULYSSES: Well, one was setting up silver tables, another was putting fine gold baskets on the tables. The third one was pouring a wine that tasted like honey . . .

PENELOPE: I wouldn't like that. I like wine to taste like wine. Where was she pouring this honeyed wine?

ULYSSES: Into cups of . . .

PENELOPE: Gold, naturally?

ULYSSES: Gold, yes. In Circe's house, the utensils are all gold or gilded.

PENELOPE: Magic is profitable! Here, I want you to replace all the gold cups with bronze.

ULYSSES: (Laughing) You'll have everything you want. Bronze cups, iron cups, even pewter, or how about the palm of your hands? Why not the palm of your beautiful hands? Come on, darling! (He goes over to her, takes one of her hands and kisses it.) How good it would be to drink from your hands!

PENELOPE: (Pulling away, disturbed) Please, Ulysses, please! Be serious!

ULYSSES: If you knew how serious, how profoundly, overwhelmingly serious I am about you right now! (He takes both her hands and kisses them greedily, one after the other.)

PENELOPE: (Pulling away again, but more gently) Control yourself, please. Not now. Did she keep her oath?

ULYSSES: An oath sworn before the gods? I'd like to have seen her not keep it!

PENELOPE: All right. Then you climbed down from the bed and went into the huge room?

ULYSSES: Huge room? What huge room?

PENELOPE: You're the one who told me about it — the huge room where your friends joined you after they had become men again.

ULYSSES: (Striking himself on the forehead) Of course, of course! That huge room! I think I must be getting tired! So, I sat down, I waited a short while, then behind Circe *(He laughs.)* the herd came in. It was the funniest thing! *(He laughs again.)*

PENELOPE: Maybe it wasn't funny for them.

ULYSSES: I'm sorry, but *(He laughs.)* seeing twenty old friends turned into pigs come trotting into a reception room — pigs, standing up on their hind legs — it's hilarious! *(He laughs again.)*

PENELOPE: I don't think it's funny, I think it's terrible.

ULYSSES: Oh, no, after ten years we'd had our fill of what was terrible. It did us good to relax. Besides, the story's almost over. She rubbed each of the pigs with a mixture . . .

PENELOPE: Their muzzles, is that what she rubbed?

ULYSSES: Their muzzles? Yes, I think so. And then one after another they dropped off the bristles covering their bodies, and they became men again. I hope you're not expecting me to narrate the scene in detail?

PENELOPE: No, no, you've said enough. If that's the way things happened.

ULYSSES: But I swore to you . . .

PENELOPE: I know you did. Did you stay long at Circe's?

ULYSSES: Until the end of the year and the return of spring. About five months.

PENELOPE: You weren't in any hurry to leave her, I must say!

ULYSSES: I was afraid of offending her and besides . . . *(Changing his approach)* Come on, old man, tell the truth. Well, at this lady's house, we ate prodigiously. There,

now you know. We had good wine, meat in abundance, and Circe engaged a cook whose talent with the ovens made her famous all over the island. Yes, yes, I know, you're thinking to yourself: what a frightful materialist! But will you try to imagine, after two years of seismic catastrophes, telluric or oceanic upheavals — in short, metaphysical anguish over the question of whether the gods are really responsible for my turmoil — how five months of materialism, desperate materialism, can be a good thing to hold onto? Don't look at me too closely, my dear: I'm afraid I got a little fat in the middle during those five months.

PENELOPE: You must really be sure of me to talk to me like that! Storyteller! Storyteller! Oh, incorrigible storyteller! But I was about to forget my main question: did you take any of the herb yourself?

ULYSSES: Herb? What herb?

PENELOPE: What do you mean, what herb? The herb for the pigs, the one Circe made your friends take.

ULYSSES: It wasn't a herb, it was a kind of drug, and an extremely suspicious one, in fact. If you watched it streaming into your glass, you felt yourself overcome with an uncontrollable sadness, a kind of deep unrest surging up from inside you. Indeed yes, I had taken it, but only after taking an antidote, a herb this time, an authentic magic herb which made Circe's drug ineffectual.

PENELOPE: How did you find out about it?

ULYSSES: From a charming young man with handsome features and light eyes whom I had met just outside the gate. He looked like that statue, you know, that statue of the god with wings on his heels —Hermes, I think it is?

PENELOPE: Perhaps it was. Hermes the nimble-footed.

ULYSSES: No, it wasn't. The gods, if they exist, have too much to do to take on human problems. *(Becoming animated)* And I'm going to tell you something, so there won't be any misunderstanding on the subject between you and me: if there really are gods, and they have left me to fend for myself, as I did, during what should have been ten of the best years of my life, then I have no use for them! Until my last breath I swear to pursue them relentlessly with my hatred! *(He controls himself, takes a deep breath, and then continues, more calmly.)* No, he was just a local boy who didn't want me to increase the numbers of the extraordinary menagerie galloping about on the grounds. So, you have the whole story. Mmmm! *(He stretches and takes a deep breath.)* What do you think of it?

PENELOPE: It's . . . very interesting, but I don't see anything in it to justify or even excuse the murder of Eurymachus and his friends. Because that's where we started, don't forget: you claimed you could demonstrate that the hardships of your life of adventure explained the rancor, indeed the murderous hatred you suddenly felt for the easy and insolent life of the suitors. I don't see that five months of carousing and gluttony reduce the injustice of an assassination perpetrated without motive.

ULYSSES: Gluttony! Carousing! You'd be wrong to see the long banquet at Circe's as a glamorous episode. My men and I . . . stocked up, that's all, we laid in reserves the way a miser hoards money, without worrying about its value. And besides, what are five puny months of gluttony compared to ten years of total deprivation?

PENELOPE: What an exaggeration! I understand that you have to tell a good tale, but let's not go too far! Whom could you convince that your ten years of wandering at sea were ten years of total deprivation? You have to deduct from that sum of years all the breaks, the holidays, the . . . interludes like the Circe episode. And God knows there were plenty!

ULYSSES: Not so many as that, not so many as that! Only, you know my temperament — when a pleasant or agreeable thing presents itself to me, in the long and painful sequence of the days of existence, my impulse compels me to jump on it and gorge myself at the expense of everything else, before chance or the malice of the gods replaces it with one of those . . . inedible bones that clutter our path. What you call "interludes" are events of this kind. As much as I may have enjoyed them, they were never more than superficial amusements.

PENELOPE: Listen to him! Such indifference, such ingratitude for . . . pleasures which, according to your own descriptions, afforded you so much joy, glory, or profit.

ULYSSES: Who said that?

PENELOPE: You did, my dear.

ULYSSES: When did I say that?

PENELOPE: Everywhere, around the Mediterranean, in the regions where, by choice or necessity, you spent time and where these things happened. With the Cicones, the Lotus Eaters, the Lestrygonians, and other inhabitants of faraway countries.

ULYSSES: *(Laughing)* Bravo, my dear, you're very good at reciting my interrupted courses and seaside holidays! Where did you learn all that?

PENELOPE: Do I have to say it again? In your legend.

ULYSSES: That's right, yes, I forgot — the old blind poet. But don't be taken in. It's not from poets that one learns the truth.

PENELOPE: But *that* poet! The powerful, the inspired, the divine! When a singer would come in the evenings, take his place at our hearth, and begin to unfurl the bright cloth of your exploits, tightly woven with the dark skein of your misfortunes, everyone believed him instantly, I first of all. And we wept.

ULYSSES: You shouldn't have. The singers, you say, arrive at the house in the evening. Simply because dinner is in the evening. They're wanderers, you see, and they know very well that their talent will win them bed and board. According to the degree of admiration they inspire in their listeners for the exploits of the hero, the degree of pity for his misfortunes, their dinner will be meager or generous and their room primitive or comfortable. So naturally they warm up to their subject and they tell a good story.

PENELOPE: *(Laughing)* What? They do it too?

ULYSSES: *(Also laughing)* They do it too! It's a profession for which I would be ideally suited. *(Returning to his story)* They tell a good story, yes, they embellish, they enhance the lies of the poet. The singers may tell good stories, but the poets simply lie.

PENELOPE: At least that's what people say.

ULYSSES: They don't say it enough! The poets lie, and seriously, because they substitute the beautiful unity of their poems for the wild dispersion of life. That's an unpardonable lie!

PENELOPE: But what about *this* poet? A magnificent poet, so simple, so gifted. He seemed to know you so well that he must have been with you for considerable stretches of time. Was he?

ULYSSES: No, that's just it. I met him, let's see — three or four times in twenty years. Let me try to remember . . . yes, that's right. Once just outside Troy, at the beginning of the war, in Agamemnon's tent, at a kind of symposium of the generals to pay our respects to the old blind poet who, by the way, was neither blind nor old at that time, but was already very skilful with the epic hexameter. I thought he was some sort of war correspondent, unusually gifted. I don't even remember who showed me the tale, signed by him, a really good tale, about a famous battle . . . But all that is so old now, so distant.

PENELOPE: What about the other times?

ULYSSES: Oh, that. It's extremely hazy. I can see him in the vicinity of Achilles' tent, the night of the hero's death. I had already tangled with Ajax over who would get the battle gear. I remember that the poet followed us around and didn't miss a word.

PENELOPE: Still young? Still clairvoyant?

ULYSSES: Who? The poet? A little less young, of course, but his eyes were still clear and bright. Then . . . *(He stops.)*

PENELOPE: Then what?

ULYSSES: Well! Then he latched onto me, he attached himself to me, following in my footsteps, narrating in detail my least acts and adventures, because, as you know, nothing was over for me. All the other Greek leaders had been back home a long time before — those that made it back — while I was still knocking valiantly about the four corners of the sterile sea. He was undoubtedly right behind me, picking up what he could. But I never saw him. *(Dreamily)* How strange it all is when you think about it! Why him? Why me? Because actually, if it hadn't been for a series of mishaps, once the war was over, I would have come straight home, and everybody would have lived happily ever after! But it took ten years. Oh, well, that's nothing. I'm not complaining. Considering the possibilities of fate, I could have come out much worse. And so could he. I think he picked the lucky number when he followed me, he had real material and the most eligible of heroes: Ulysses of the thousand tricks. The undauntable! The incredible! The champion of endurance! But you must never forget that the poet has his truth and I have mine.

PENELOPE: And that there is a third truth, the real one, that we will never know because neither he nor you will tell it.

ULYSSES: I'm telling it right now.

PENELOPE: Like the storyteller you are.

ULYSSES: No, it's almost unadorned, with just the bare ornament I have to add now that I'm back in a better world, so I can stand to face what I'm telling. *(Pause)*

PENELOPE: Be careful, Ulysses! Don't think I'm convinced because you've answered my questions skillfully. My arguments still stand, but you present yours with such charm . . . ah, you're exactly like my memory of you: a charmer. Formidable.

ULYSSES: *(Smiling)* I thought I was a storyteller.

PENELOPE: *(Laughing)* One doesn't preclude the other. You are a charming storyteller. And woe to whoever gets closer than three steps away from you. He succumbs, he expires, he . . . becomes your plaything.

ULYSSES: Is that why you're staying so far away from me? *(He starts over toward her.)*

PENELOPE: *(Backing up quickly)* No, please, stay where you are! Leave me my lucidity so I can see clearly how I managed without you, living without you when I was lonely, and the women of the island came to call on me, one by one.

ULYSSES: You never told me that. They came to see you?

PENELOPE: Almost every day, one after another. They must have organized a visiting marathon and assigned days. God! I think they were measuring the progressive ravages of solitude and sorrow that were pushing me day by day toward old age and decrepitude!

ULYSSES: That's hard to imagine. What did they say?

PENELOPE: Not much. They examined me very closely, shamelessly, they . . . scrutinized me, all the while politely announcing whole collections of catastrophes and violent deaths of Greek leaders or warriors. Then they talked about you, in lavish terms, the kind one heaps on the widows or almost-widows or soon-to-be widows of soldiers: "I say, my dear, it seems your husband is doing magnificent things out there. They say he's won such and such a strategic battle, pulled off such and such a brilliant maneuver, etc., etc." What they mean is: "But if *my* husband, who was obliged to remain here to attend to business, if *he* had been there instead of yours, he would have done much better, I have no doubt of it!"

ULYSSES: That's what they were like?

PENELOPE: They were ten times worse . . . *(Controlling herself)* No, let's be fair. I'll have to admit, there *was* the horse! The horse got them all right! It astounded them! It did me too, for that matter.

ULYSSES: Oh, really? And what horse was that?

PENELOPE: What do you mean, what horse was that? The Trojan horse! *(Suddenly worried)* It *was* you who invented it?

ULYSSES: *(Laughing)* Oh, yes, don't worry. I didn't build it, but I did have the idea for it. How could I have forgotten that horse! *(He laughs.)* It was really something, you know, a sort of gigantic toy, a toy for grown-ups, harmless in appearance but stuffed with armed Greek soldiers, hand-picked and highly skilled. I was in there myself.

PENELOPE: It was dangerous.

ULYSSES: Not really. You just have to know the people you're dealing with. I had made a bet with myself that the Trojans would not be capable, in fact, absolutely incapable, of muzzling their curiosity, and that they would dismantle a portion of their fortress wall to get the horse into the city rather than leave it outside. And I won! They worked together like an efficient giant! The Greek army had hardly had time to re-embark, pretending to return home, when the wall of Troy fell into rubble from the picks of the demolition crew. After which the horse was led in in triumph by the whole population *(He laughs.)*, His Majesty the horse, treated with such dignity, pomp, and pride that when I think about it again I could just die laughing. Anyway, the horse and the Greek army entered Troy. *(He bursts out laughing.)* I'm sorry, my dear, but that story about the horse will always be one of my favorites. *(Pause. He continues, serious again.)* But who would ever have believed that that famous war, a war of ten long years, would end with a fluke, a comic episode?

PENELOPE: And who would ever have believed that I, Penelope, only yesterday a nice, unimportant girl, would suddenly find myself placed on a pedestal and transformed into the object of admiration and even desire, or at least somewhat brutal envy, though generally flattering, of all the eligible young men of the island? Who, especially, would have believed that once Ulysses was back home, after twenty years finally back home with her, she would still feel so alone? Alone! Always under siege, always . . . exposed, but to what? What is it? *(Pause. She takes two steps toward Ulysses.)* Oh, Ulysses, dear Ulysses, try to understand me, and make me understand you. You're here, standing before me, like another man, one I don't know, that I'll have to learn to know. Since your return, I've been struggling against a frightful thing, and I know you feel it as much as I do: the essence of life, its flower, its rose, nothing will ever be able to return it to us so we can give it to each other, through the grace of our union, nothing, not even your wizardry. We were strangers the day of our wedding; we're doubly strangers the day of our reunion. We have nothing in common but a few minor faults, a few . . . flaws of character that we've been eagerly calling to mind for an hour. That's not enough to fill twenty years of absence. The great temperate region in the middle of life is missing and will always be missing. Just think! When I was twenty, at the height of my youth, you had already been away at war for two years. And what a war! An absurd war that you didn't want to fight in, that you absolutely refused to fight in! Through the memory of my tears, I can still hear the furious shouting of Agamemnon when he came here to try to get you to go with him to Troy. And you defended yourself! How you defended yourself! Ah! I admired you so much, you know. But finally you had to leave. You went off to war and, my God, how good you were at it, that's the terrible thing. You even liked it. You liked it so much that after two or three years, you had become the cleverest, the shrewdest, the most skillful of the Greek soldiers, the one everybody knew better than to tangle with. More formidable than Achilles! More dangerous than Ajax! A real prodigy, weren't you? You never stopped inventing, scheming, hatching plots, for pleasure, setting traps that the enemy always walked into, that he seemed to rush into voluntarily. That's how you earned your nickname of the man of a thousand tricks, the name that distinguishes you, paints your portrait, and will remain with you. You know, it's frightful, but one might say that you had been waiting for the war, that you had to have it to complete your personality. *(Changing moods, speaking directly)* What are you doing?

(Ulysses has got up and gone over to the bed.)

ULYSSES: Nothing. I'm looking for a blanket *(He fumbles around with the covers.)* because you make me cold, my dear, you freeze me down to the bone. *(He covers his shoulders.)*

PENELOPE: It had to be said, Ulysses, but it's true that the saying is painful. A moment ago, for example, when you remembered your fight with Ajax over Achilles' battle gear, I shivered from head to foot. Achilles' battle gear, Ulysses, what difference does it make? Is it possible that a man —a real man — could fight another

31

man over such a minute question as the ownership of the trappings, however fine they might be, of a dead war hero?

ULYSSES: *(His head lowered)* Yes, yes, you're right. It was childish.

PENELOPE: And what did I do here, all alone, while you were at war? Well, I finished becoming myself, all alone here; I took on my woman's form and my role as a wife. I developed all alone, always all alone. Ah! You don't know what it's like! All the little secrets that people say a woman confides to her husband, her lover, to a man anyway, insignificant secrets, naturally, but that matter to her, I had to confide them to myself alone, always all alone, as I discovered them, with no illusions that they could interest anyone. Not even me. Since these discoveries are made gradually, one at a time, it's never really tragic. Except on the rare occasions when one of them coincides with a date that for one reason or another you consider important. I remember the morning of my thirtieth birthday. I had gotten up without even thinking about it, but around ten o'clock . . . *(She changes her mind.)* No, what good would it do? *(She sighs.)* I'm already eight years older. *(She lowers her head and holds it with both hands.)*

ULYSSES: *(Quietly)* I'm listening to you, Penelope darling, oh! I'm listening to you. It's all I can give you, but I'm listening to you with all my soul.

PENELOPE: *(Straightening up)* Sometimes you get crazy ideas . . . sudden urges to . . . to do what, exactly? I remember a summer day, don't ask me what year.

I just know that it was very hot, too hot. Not a breath of air. All I had on was a plain white dress.

ULYSSES: Which one?

PENELOPE: You don't know it. I didn't have it when you were here.

ULYSSES: What was it like?

PENELOPE: Very short, above the knee, sleeveless, with a low V-neck — the standard summer dress. Light as a feather.

ULYSSES: It sounds to me as if you were practically naked . . .

PENELOPE: It was extremely hot.

ULYSSES: *(Faltering)* But still . . .

PENELOPE: The suitors had been after me for months to preside at one of their dinners, and I had promised that I would. I came down around seven o'clock and was welcomed, as you might imagine, by endless smiles and cheers and flattery. They all outdid themselves.

ULYSSES: And you, naturally, bowed very low, in acknowledgement.

PENELOPE: I don't know what I did. I just remember the heat, like a steam bath. I felt the sweat running down between my breasts. Can you imagine that?

ULYSSES: *(Dryly)* As if I were there.

PENELOPE: I had put my finger in the front placket of my dress, to keep the material away from my skin — like this, you see? *(She demonstrates on her nightgown.)* Suddenly—how did it come about? I've often tried to put myself back into that state, but it's always been impossible.

ULYSSES: *(Shouting)* For God's sake, go on!

PENELOPE: *(Enjoying his discomfort)*

What's the matter with you?

ULYSSES: Nothing unusual. Go on.

PENELOPE: Suddenly — how can I describe it? All the suitors simply . . . disappeared, at least to my eyes. I don't remember exactly where I was sitting at the table . . .

ULYSSES: Well, I do. On your right was Antinous and on your left, "poor" Eurymachus.

PENELOPE: How do you know?

ULYSSES: (Shouting) Because I know everything! Then what happened? Then what?

PENELOPE: (Becoming animated) I blotted them all out of my mind. The desire, no, it was stronger than desire, the need had seized me to take off my dress, to finish the gesture that my index finger had begun, to pop off the first button, then the second, and then the others, like picking grapes, until finally the dress would fall off and I'd be naked . . .

ULYSSES: (In a rage) You didn't do that?

PENELOPE: (Continuing) . . . completely naked, so this assembly of blurred faces could see the real woman they were quarreling over . . .

ULYSSES: (Rushing over to her) I'm asking you if you did that! (He grabs her arm and she pulls away.)

PENELOPE: (Continuing) . . . the real woman, unadorned, naked, not just a convenient means of acquiring by marriage our land, our possessions, our power.

ULYSSES: Answer me, I order you . . . I beg you. I know you're capable of doing that, on impulse, one of those impulses . . .

But did you do it?

(Pause)

PENELOPE: (Slowly) I wanted to do it so badly, so desperately, I had to hold myself back with such immense effort not to do it that I swear to you, it's as if I had done it.

ULYSSES: (Relieved) Yes, but you didn't do it! (He takes a deep breath.)

(Pause)

PENELOPE: Maybe it would have been better if I had done it.

ULYSSES: Don't talk nonsense.

PENELOPE: A hundred times afterward I've thought about it. Some nights I still think about it. Let's see, I say to myself, let's see now, what this act would really have brought about. And I picture myself — can you picture me, Ulysses, a naked woman on the table, lying on the table with the overturned cups, broken plates, spilled wine? (Ulysses coughs.) And around her, a hundred brutish beasts, a hundred wild beasts mad with desire, all snorting? What would they have ended up doing, Ulysses? Tell me that, you who know everything.

ULYSSES: (Tonelessly) And what about you, Penelope, what would you have ended up doing? Tell me that.

PENELOPE: (After a pause) To be honest, I have no idea.

ULYSSES: Well, I do. You would have stood up again, you would have put your dress back on, calmly . . .

PENELOPE: Calmly!

ULYSSES: . . . you would have brushed off the crumbs, sponged the wine stains with a wet napkin, and then you would have said, in your woman-of-the-world voice,

"Forgive me, gentlemen, this was all a simple error. Do me the honor of ignoring it." Isn't that true? Isn't it? Think about it. *(Anxiously)* Isn't it true? *(He tries to laugh.)*

PENELOPE: *(After a pause, seriously)* I have no idea.

ULYSSES: Of course you do!

PENELOPE: No, I swear to you. *(She breathes deeply.)* It would be misleading to think that a good woman — I mean a woman who cultivates goodness, as I do, for example, not without a certain ostentation — it would be very misleading to believe that that woman will remain good, rigidly good, unfailingly and consistently good, good once and for all, throughout her life. So it is with me, as I've told you . . .

ULYSSES: *(Interrupting her)* No, don't talk about it! I know all that, I can sense it. But please, don't talk about it!

PENELOPE: Why not? For once, a man is about to obtain a full confession from a woman . . .

ULYSSES: No! I couldn't bear . . . I'm sure I couldn't bear the sight, even imaginary, of your . . . of this . . . *(He searches for the right word.)* Exposure.

PENELOPE: A degrading exposure, in your opinion?

ULYSSES: Leave morality out of it! That's not the point, the point is that it's physically impossible *(He grinds his teeth.)*, it's impossible, impossible to bear. Intolerable, that's the word.

(Pause)

PENELOPE: And what about you, Ulysses?

ULYSSES: What do you mean, what about me?

PENELOPE: If you had been in the banquet hall, let's say, mingling with the suitors, one of them, how would you have reacted to this woman?

ULYSSES: Immediately, without reflection, no matter what it might cost me later, I'll tell you exactly what I feel since we're being brutally honest. *(Very straightforward)* I would have leapt on you and carried you off to my room!

PENELOPE: Do you think the others would have let you do it?

ULYSSES: I would have fought them off.

PENELOPE: One against a hundred?

ULYSSES: That's about what I did this morning.

PENELOPE: That's about what you did during your long crusade, every time you were faced with a . . . an exposure of a naked woman, except that it wasn't *your* room you rushed off to, it was the woman's.

ULYSSES: But that never . . .

PENELOPE: Come now, don't deny it. I have proof. By the way, I'd like to invite one of your women to spend a few days with us. I'd like to question her.

ULYSSES: You what? Which woman?

PENELOPE: The one who was, I believe, the most cherished.

ULYSSES: Ah? And who was that?

PENELOPE: Calypso, of course.

ULYSSES: *(Stupefied)* Calypso! Oh, good God, there she is again! I thought she was far away, but there she is in flesh and blood. I'm warning you right now that I won't receive her in your presence. I'll disappear.

PENELOPE: I'll manage. I have an idea she and I will get on very well together.

ULYSSES: In the first place, she won't accept the invitation.

PENELOPE: Would you like to bet?

ULYSSES: She's not an easy guest to please, you know. She's very particular about food.

PENELOPE: Oh, I'll inform myself on her tastes. And surely you won't let me down by "disappearing" before you tell me about her habits in the matter of . . . lodging? On this question my intuition can hardly replace your experience.

ULYSSES: (As if to himself) What is this, for God's sake? And to think that I believed Calypso was forgotten, at the other end of the world! (To Penelope) All right, I'm ready to tell you everything you want to ask me.

PENELOPE: Everything, really?

ULYSSES: Absolutely everything. It won't even be worth inviting her. What do you want me to admit to you?

PENELOPE: Oh, very little really. What you did with Calypso.

ULYSSES: A fine question! I wept all the time.

PENELOPE: Not all the time!

ULYSSES: Yes, all the time, from morning to night.

PENELOPE: All right, but what about from night to morning?

ULYSSES: (Impatiently) Be careful, you're going to become impossible!

PENELOPE: Ah! So I'm the one?

ULYSSES: (Violently) No, I am and I know it! But if you knew how exhausting this kind of . . . interrogation can be! I'm always thinking it's over with once and for all. Exactly what is it that you want to know? If I made love to her? Well, the answer is yes! A hundred times yes! And I did it the best I could. And I liked it as much as she did. But that didn't keep me from being faithful to you, from thinking of you constantly, from wanting more than anything else in the world to come back to Ithaca where I am right now. And nothing else counts. So there! Besides . . .

PENELOPE: Besides what?

ULYSSES: I told Calypso that. I told her twenty times, very clearly.

PENELOPE: Possibly.

ULYSSES: No. Positively.

PENELOPE: But you told her something else too.

ULYSSES: I may have. I told her plenty of stories.

PENELOPE: No, no, not a story: you talked to her about me.

ULYSSES: About you? You think I did that?

PENELOPE: Absolutely. Here's what you said: "As nice as she is, Penelope would be insignificant and plain compared to you."

ULYSSES: (Flabbergasted) I said that?

PENELOPE: In so many words.

ULYSSES: I couldn't have. What are your sources?

PENELOPE: Do you have to ask?

ULYSSES: (Annoyed) Oh! The old blind poet again? What business is it of his?

PENELOPE: I would remind you of one thing: to receive a piece of information like this . . .

ULYSSES: What information?

PENELOPE: What we're discussing — the opinion you hold of me and that you confided to that woman . . .

ULYSSES: *(Shouting)* It's not true, I never said that! At least, not in those words.

PENELOPE: We'll let that pass. So, to receive this information out of the blue, one evening before the fire, with the entire household, serving girls, nurse, herdsmen, everyone gathered around the singer standing there in the light of the fire, calmly reciting the poem about you, it makes quite an impression, as you might imagine. It's like . . . fate speaking.

ULYSSES: I realize that, but I still say . . .

PENELOPE: *(Interrupting him)* It was Phemius, our singer, who let me in on the facts, without realizing it, poor man.

ULYSSES: That jackass! What business is it of his either? To think that he almost got it this morning. If it hadn't been for Telemachus who put in a good word for him, I would have finished him off with the others. My God, if I'd known, he'd be down reciting Homer to the moles right now!

PENELOPE: Don't act more spiteful than you really are.

ULYSSES: I'm not. Don't you think he could have remembered what was in the poem and left that passage out before he went stumbling into it?

PENELOPE: One feels very stupid, you see, disarmed, vulnerable and . . . the blow strikes straight to the heart. Then you should see — ha! you should see the servants put on their insolent good manners!

You should see them pretending they didn't hear a thing, but not pretending too hard, so the Mistress won't get the idea that they really didn't hear anything. And then there's the singer who suddenly realizes something is wrong with the audience. He wonders if he hasn't just made a blunder without realizing it. He gets confused, he breaks the mood, he loses his place, then he begins to stammer. The whole thing ends in hideous embarrassment, an awkwardness so thick you could cut it with a knife.

ULYSSES: Phemius is a fool, and I'll tell him so the first chance I get. But he's not the only one. There's always our eternal old blind fool. Until now I thought he was fairly harmless, but I . . . *(Forcefully)* Never, do you hear me, never did I say those words. You believe me, don't you?

PENELOPE: Yes, yes, I believe you.

ULYSSES: Those words are his invention, not mine.

PENELOPE: *(Unconcerned)* I'm convinced of that.

ULYSSES: "Insignificant and plain!" Now I ask you! I who spent my time extolling to my hosts my wife's beauty and her regal bearing!

PENELOPE: Don't worry about it. It's an old incident, absorbed a long time ago.

ULYSSES: These poets are shameless! They say anything, and everybody believes them and even believes them so strongly that between two versions of the same event, one simply real and the other poetic, it's always the poetic one that people choose.

PENELOPE: It's the power of legend.

ULYSSES: *(With sudden concern)* Don't say it like that!

PENELOPE: Like what?

ULYSSES: I don't know — you act as if it doesn't matter.

PENELOPE: Isn't that what you want?

ULYSSES: Yes, but not like that, not with that smile, not in that light, bantering, worldly way! No, that's not what I want. *(Very irritated)* That's not it at all. *(He paces up and down.) (Pause)*

PENELOPE: By the way, now that I'm thinking of it — how long did you stay with Calypso?

ULYSSES: Here we go again! After the reign of Circe, now we have the empire of Calypso. Who's after Calypso?

PENELOPE: I'm waiting for your answer.

ULYSSES: It's getting better every time! First we're a husband and wife discussing love and marriage and then a defendant and a lawyer engaged in cross-examination. The court is back in session! *(Changing moods)* I really don't know, my dear. Let's say . . . an indefinite time, an unverified amount of time.

PENELOPE: In months or in years?

ULYSSES: In years, of course, in years. Perhaps six or seven.

PENELOPE: *(Dumfounded)* Six or seven years?!

ULYSSES: More or less, more or less.

PENELOPE: But that's horrifying! I find it . . . horrifying. When you left for the war, twenty years ago, you and I had a total of two years of married life. Only two years, do you realize that? If you stayed with Calypso three times longer than you did with me, she's the one you should have returned to, not to me. She's your real wife!

ULYSSES: Don't talk nonsense!

PENELOPE: I'd never thought of that. She's your real wife. Was she good to you?

ULYSSES: Oh, you know, it's always the same with those women. They save you from a shipwreck, they take you in, they feed and clothe you, but then you have to pay for it. *(Wearily)* She had me making love to her every night, sometimes more than once or twice, sometimes during the day! On that schedule you can imagine! . . . She claimed it rejuvenated me, but I could tell I was falling apart, going downhill, I could hardly stand up. If she hadn't told me one day that she was giving in, that I could leave and she would furnish the materials to make a raft — I've never known why — I would have died there in her service.

(Pause)

PENELOPE: *(Quietly)* What a joke! What an inept, idiotic, stupid joke! *(Sudden outburst)* What a farce! *(Quietly again)* Perhaps we will be cited in the future, Ulysses and I, as perfect mates — an exemplary couple. The woman of the couple was irreproachable, aside from a few daydreams that never surfaced into the real world. The woman was faithful, a bit childishly faithful, to the point of inventing games to safeguard her faithfulness, like the tapestry, for example. The man, Ulysses, was a hero, a conqueror of men. A conqueror of women too, when he had no other choice, but on the whole, he was also faithful. The proof is that when he wasn't making love, he was crying like a baby. He sighed, he sobbed, he hiccupped, he shed torrents of tears over the memory of his beloved wife — the one with the tapestry — his father, his son, his herdsman, his foreman, his nurse, and other familiar personalities in the house on Ithaca. But his tears, even buckets of them, never prevented him from carrying out brilliantly his mission as a man with numerous island princesses, in order to thank them for the favors they had done him. Is that simple enough? Pure enough? Beautiful enough? And don't forget the warning of the greatest poet of the Greek nation: naturally, life, real life, always has a headstart on the poet, but he follows it, faithfully, so faithfully that everybody in the story is faithful. When his great genial hand has recorded the death of the suitors and the reunion of the exemplary couple, we can then be assured of possessing an extraordinary poem — something to recite, to sing, at social gatherings, in the evening, before the fire, for thousands of years. But in the meantime, as I said before, what a farce! What a wretched, tragic, ridiculous farce! *(She throws herself face down on the bed and hides her head in her hands.)*

ULYSSES: *(Melancholy)* You refuse to understand. *(He begins pacing.)* I could talk·myself blue in the face, she'd never understand. *(He turns to Penelope.)* Penelope, only this morning, in the big hall downstairs *(He points at the floor.)*, I carried out one of the hardest battles, maybe the hardest, of my life, without a trace of comedy. I was totally sincere. That doesn't touch you? It doesn't move you?

PENELOPE: You could have avoided it. Eurymachus told you a way.

ULYSSES: Three or four times during that battle, I felt myself close to defeat. A deadly panic seized me, a loosening of control, the sudden feeling of my weakness, my age faced with the inexhaustible strength of a hundred young men. I'm not twenty years old anymore, as you know. I'm past the age of thirsting after compliments, but I hunger for justice. And you, Penelope, are unjust. I swear that what I did this morning deserves neither your mockery nor, even less, your disapproval. I almost lost. There were only four of us — me, Telemachus, Eumaeus, and Philoetius. Four against a hundred. Four men against a hundred men! That's worth something in itself.

PENELOPE: Against these hundred men, I was alone. And I sincerely believe I would have preferred having to defend myself against their swords and javelins than against their smiles and gifts. Alone, yes, against a hundred young men, some of them very good-looking — dic you have time to see that, before you killed them? *I saw them, but I never looked at them.* That too is worth something in itself.

(Pause)

ULYSSES: *(Gently)* Aren't both of us worth something in ourselves? *(He goes over to Penelope, who is now sitting up on the bed.)* And even more together? *(He sits down by her.)*

PENELOPE: Oh, Ulysses, tell me what has happened. What has happened? What has crept in between us, silently, all these years? *(Insistently)* Tell me what it is, Ulysses, tell me!

ULYSSES: How could I know? *(He puts his arm around his wife's shoulders.)* Life, I suppose. Perhaps it was simply life. *(Pause)*

PENELOPE: There are times when whatever separates us seems to me almost nothing at all. And other times when it seems to me so substantial, so . . . gigantic, that it's as if we lived in different worlds. But whether it's a grain of salt or a mountain, it separates us. Oh, Ulysses, I've lost the sense I used to have of seeing things through your eyes, touching things with your hands, loving things with your heart. And that's why I've lost hope. My own eyes, my hands, my heart have suddenly come into being; I've only felt their existence since yesterday. I don't know how to use them yet. During the last twenty years, without you, I only learned to live with you. How will I learn, and where will I learn, to live without you?

ULYSSES: I don't know. I don't know at all, but I understand what you're saying. Yet I was convinced, during those twenty years, that in spite of everything, above all else, I was your husband, the one you had chosen, the one man in the world that you wanted.

PENELOPE: You *were* my husband, Ulysses, you still are, but that doesn't mean the same thing it used to, as it did yesterday, when I had not seen you again.

ULYSSES: I've disappointed you.

PENELOPE: No, it's not that. How can I make you understand? *(She searches for the right words.)* Inside me I had . . . there were . . . yes, that's it, a set of hooks, ready to slip into a matching set inside you, in a flash, just like that. But I know now *(Insistently),* I know I won't slip into anything. I won't find anything inside you to slip into anymore. It's useless to try, we have to see things as they are: something has gone, something has slammed shut, something irreparable. *(Directly to Ulysses)* Everything you say, everything you do shocks me, offends me, irritates me. We may as well tell the truth.

ULYSSES: Yes, we may as well tell the truth. But I had noticed anyway. *(They look at each other for a moment, very close together. Then Ulysses removes his arm from his wife's shoulders and gets up.)* I think we're going to have to be brave, again. I've been given a . . . strange mission, but what isn't strange in this world?

PENELOPE: Who gave you this mission?

ULYSSES: A man named Tiresias, you don't know him. I'm supposed to go from city to city carrying a polished oar, and keep walking, not stopping anywhere, until I come to people who have never heard of the sea.

PENELOPE: People who have never heard of the sea! Do such people exist?

ULYSSES: Apparently they do. Then, someone who has never seen an oar . . .

PENELOPE: You'll never find him!

ULYSSES: I've found odder things than that. This person, whom I will encounter, will ask me why I'm carrying a winnowing fan over my shoulder. My answer will be to plant the oar in the ground. And that's all, it'll be over. Mission accomplished.

(Pause)

PENELOPE: That doesn't sound very hard . . . or very long . . . or very dangerous.

ULYSSES: Hm! I'm not so sure. Coming back home after the war didn't sound very hard or very long or very dangerous either. But you see what it has cost us.

PENELOPE: That's true, my God, it's true! *(She suddenly starts crying.)*

ULYSSES: Don't be upset — I'm shrewd, you know! The man of a thousand tricks! Ulysses the schemer! The hero of endurance! I hope he'll leave me in peace this time.

PENELOPE: Who?

ULYSSES: Who else? The old blind man! The old blind poet!

PENELOPE: Do you think he's still alive?

ULYSSES: The blind man? I've always been told that pests like that never die. But I'd better not find him on my path again! Or if I do, he'd better renew his stock of epithets! *(Returning to his mission)* Once the oar is planted in the ground, I can leave, the way I understand it, `come home, back here with . . . with you *(Penelope sobs.)* to live out my life to a happy old age . . . and then to a gentle death which, I think he said, will come to me from the sea.

PENELOPE: What does that mean?

ULYSSES: How should I know? Perhaps it's a symbol.

PENELOPE: Yes . . . so you're to be the eternal wanderer?

ULYSSES: That's the way it seems, yes, that's the way it seems . . .

PENELOPE: Oh, Ulysses! *(They rush into each other's arms and embrace passionately. Pause. Then they let go of each other. Penelope continues, her voice unsteady.)* When do you plan to leave?

ULYSSES: I don't know exactly. Shall we say — tomorrow?

PENELOPE: Let's say tomorrow.

(He goes slowly toward the door at the back, stops, and turns around.)

ULYSSES: Tomorrow morning?

PENELOPE: Tomorrow morning.

(Ulysses opens the door while the lights go down.)

Moses and the Mountain

ASCENSION DU SINAI

Characters, in order of appearance:

Aaron
Moses
Nadab
Abihu
Ahisamac
Ruben
Manasseh
Simeon
The Apparitor
Jigal
Hosea
Sodi
Guenel
Caleb
Dan
Gaddi
Shammna
Shapbath
Palthi
Gaddiel
Sethur
Nachbi
Workmen
A Messenger
First Man
Second Man
A Crowd
Four Statue-bearers

Moses and the Mountain

ACT I

The scene reveals the inside of a tent (at the foot of Mt. Sinai) — a rather simple setting. There is an opening in the backdrop. A camper's cot and two or three chairs.

As the curtain rises, Aaron, younger brother of Moses, is standing, half facing the audience. Moses is standing, his back to the audience, about three-fourths hidden by a folding screen in the left back corner of the stage. One guesses that he is washing himself.

A short time passes. Gentle splashes of water can be heard behind the screen. Aaron sighs, apparently recovering from a bit of unpleasant daydreaming. A prey to his thoughts, he takes a few steps downstage, stops for a minute, glances toward the folding screen, then slowly returns to his original place.

AARON: Moses!

MOSES: Yes?

AARON: Listen, I don't see it. I just have to admit it, I don't see it at all.

(Moses does not answer. Soft splashes of water are heard.) Do you hear what I'm saying? (Louder) I don't see it at all.

MOSES: You don't have a thing to do with it. The matter concerns me.

AARON: But I'm your brother.

MOSES: Okay, but my brother is not me, and this concerns me — and me alone.

AARON: (Heaving a sigh, he goes slowly to the door of the tent and looks outside.) It's terrible weather. Moses, you hear me? Really awful weather!

41

MOSES: *(Calmly)* Yes, it's always that way.

AARON: What's that way?

MOSES: The weather . . . things like that. Every time, it's the same story. Every time I've tried to do something just a little bit unusual, the weather, the wind, the heat or the cold—everything opposed me. I think the elements try to discourage people who lack self-assurance.

AARON: Do you lack self-assurance?

MOSES: *(Laughing)* What do you think? *(Changing his tone)* Say!

AARON: What?

MOSES: Want to scrub my back?

AARON: *(He obeys.)* Why, you aren't washing yourself, Moses, you're . . . scouring yourself.

MOSES: In order to go where I'm going, you have to be spotless. Scrub harder, don't be afraid! Spotless within as well as without.

AARON: Without, sure, but how do you get spotless within?

MOSES: I haven't eaten a bite in twenty-four hours.

AARON: *(With irony)* Great! You're going to be in fine·shape to go up that filthy mountain.

MOSES: I'm stronger than people think. *(A short time passes. Moses dries himself.)* There! That's fine. Hand me my tunic. Thanks. *(One can see him putting on his tunic, a type of long white smock which hangs to his knees. After he is dressed, he walks from behind the folding screen where the tin tub used for his bath can be seen and sits down.)* People don't bathe enough. I like that feeling of total cleanliness . . . yes, total cleanliness . . . Why is it so dreary?

AARON: I just told you. The weather is lousy. *(He goes back to the door.)* Just look at that rain cloud! It looks like an immense sea falling down from the sky. The mountain is drowning in it.

MOSES: *(Joining him at the door)* It's not a rain cloud, Aaron, it's a storm cloud.

AARON: What's the difference?

MOSES: A rain cloud is a sort of product of the weather, a very natural and ordinary product—like rain, fog, or ice on a winter's day. A storm cloud is something quite different — at least I see it as different. It doesn't just appear; somebody makes it appear.

AARON: Who?

MOSES: All right, look! See that mist rolling into a ball and then stretching out — almost flexing its muscles. You'd think it was alive. Well, it is alive—definitely. Little by little it encircles everything. Look, look at it. In fifteen minutes, even Mt. Sinai will be hidden by it. *(Forcefully)* All that is controlled. There's someone back of it all. Someone is concealed in it.

AARON: Who? Who's hiding in it?

MOSES: *(With a bit of fear in his voice)* Look at that mist. *(A short time passes. The two watch the mist.)*

AARON: Listen, don't go up there.

MOSES: *(Smiling)*.Why not?

AARON: It's dangerous. *(Seriously)* It is, Moses, I assure you. It's extremely dangerous.

MOSES: What isn't dangerous in the

world we live in?

AARON: You know what that rain cloud . . . that storm cloud reminds me of? A trap — that's it, a . . . a clever trap to deceive the naïve.

MOSES: And I am naïve?

AARON: You're, how shall I say it? You're so gullible that people make of you whatever they wish.

MOSES: For example?

AARON: All right, Wednesday morning, when Zipporah, your wife, came back from the market . . . *(Changing his tone)* But, *look* at that! It's lighting up! And it's glowing! What's happening? Just look! *Look!* Now the storm cloud is glowing from within . . . glowing from the inside. See? Do you see that?

MOSES: *(Calmly)* I see it clearly.

AARON: But who could be making a fire way up there, all alone, on a winter's night like this? A woodcutter, maybe?

MOSES: Do you think a woodcutter's fire would cast such a bright light? Such an intense light? For all my gullibility, I refuse to accept the explanation. That fire, you realize . . *(He stops suddenly.)*

AARON: *(Impatiently)* Well?

MOSES: . . . is not a natural fire. I mean —one kindled and kept by human hands. It's a fire, well, a fire that's . . .

AARON: Supernatural?

MOSES: I didn't dare say it, but that's what I was thinking. *(Pause. The two men stand pensively.)*

AARON: Supernatural or not, someone had to start it. Who?

MOSES: Starting it is nothing; what mat-

ters is keeping it burning . . . giving it enough wood to make it glow with a truly extraordinary brightness. *(A short time passes.)* Shall I tell you? That's more than a fire, it's a fire-place . . . yes, a place of light and heat which both attracts and warms us.

AARON: *(As in a dream)* It's possible.

MOSES: It's certain. Besides, I'll see for myself.

AARON: What do you mean, you'll see for yourself?

MOSES: Surely I'll pass it on the way up the mountain, and I'll examine it.

AARON: You'll find nothing at all! Do you believe for a moment that I'm going to let my brother face the dangers of that crafty mountain which bursts forth in flames without anybody knowing why? You're staying here.

MOSES: I must go up there.

AARON: You're not budging.

MOSES: I will go! And I'll scale the slopes of that mountain until someone tells me to stop.

AARON: And if nobody says anything?

MOSES: I'll reach the summit and start down the other side, until . . .

AARON: *(Interrupting him)* Moses, you're mad! You're stark raving mad! Snow is up there! Ice is up there! And in order to get there, you'll surely have to overcome obstacles that neither you nor anybody else can imagine: passes, cliffs, crags . . . not to mention wild animals.

MOSES: What wild animals?

AARON: Those that are up there.

MOSES: Some are up there? That's news

43

to me . . . unless you're including among your wild animals some rabbits or hares, squirrels, foxes . . . or maybe, at worst, one of those little wolf-cubs that run and play like puppies.

AARON: And the bears? The brown ones? The black ones? The grizzlies?

MOSES: There are no bears up there.

AARON: Really? *(A short time passes. Then, softening)* Moses, I tremble when I see you so sure of yourself, so self-confident, for when danger leaps across your path, you'll be so astonished that you'll hand yourself over, bound hand and foot, without making so much as a gesture in your own defense.

MOSES: Must I repeat that up there I'll be in no kind of danger? I have been ordered to climb the slopes of that mountain and, once up there, to wait, that's all. Thus, I must do it, Aaron. Thus, I will do it.

AARON: Who ordered you to do that?

MOSES: *(Exasperated)* Ah! Are we really going to rehash what we've said a dozen times? *(Very distinctly)* The one who gave me this order to climb Mt. Sinai is my Lord, and yours, the Lord of all men, and of all beasts and of all things, the Lord God, as He calls Himself. Is that clear enough? Yes, good! And on that note, allow me to finish getting dressed, Aaron. It's already daybreak. It's high time I left.

(A short time passes. He begins to dress rapidly, but carefully, in silence, at first, then responding to Aaron's comments.)

AARON: *(After a long silence)* Forgive me for insisting, but I can't help it. I find it . . . insane.

MOSES: Not again!

AARON: Yes, again! And always! Suddenly, I realize that you're going to leave. Do you understand that, Moses . . . that you're about to leave me? The imminence of your departure makes it real . . . dramatic. I see it as if I were there. One can't imagine all that could happen along a mountain trail!

MOSES: And can you imagine all that could happen to a man in his bed, Aaron? *(In a softer tone)* Say, will you straighten the sash on my cloak? It's caught somewhere. *(Aaron obeys.)* Thanks. You notice that I'm not taking this journey lightly. I don't trust cold weather, and I'm not anxious to return with a case of bronchitis.

AARON: When will you come back? *If* you come back.

MOSES: I haven't the vaguest idea. I just imagine that as soon as I have done what is expected of me, no one will detain me.

AARON: How can you be so naïve? Maybe you *do* imagine that, but have you observed that with the . . . the Lord God, things always turn out just the opposite of what people expect?

MOSES: *(Sharply)* Aaron!

AARON: What?

MOSES: You're blaspheming.

AARON: Me? Not in the least. I'm only exercising the faculty for observation which I received at birth. Let's see now, sincerely, can you deny that this . . . this Lord God is, most of the time, a . . . rather strange fellow?

MOSES: Careful, Aaron!

44

AARON: Why? If He hears me, He knows very well that I'm telling the truth. Yes, a very odd fellow. Here, when you think He's far away, but right here, very close, breathing down your neck and appearing to you so suddenly that He makes you jump nearly out of your skin. Away, when you think He's near and you want to talk to Him, but away like no one in the world is away — miles and miles away and separated from you by a kind of opaque, uncrossable desert, so that if you call Him, your voice strikes against a wall and comes back at you like a slap in the face. Wrathful without anybody knowing what the devil could have provoked His wrath, and then suddenly loving, blessing, promising rewards in this world or in the other; never truly happy, always in a bad mood and punishing you for sins you haven't even had time to think of committing. And that's the . . . man who charged you with your mission . . . *(More direct)* Have you ever seen Him?

MOSES: No, I never see Him, but He talks to me.

AARON: Does He now? Well, I, who as a Levite, should be closer to religious matters than you, I confess to you that not only have I never seen Him, but I have never even *heard* Him.

MOSES: Is that possible?

AARON: Would I lie to you? To give me orders, He uses the indirect approach: through a dream, memory, signs, coincidence. But never have I had the honor of hearing His voice. How does it happen?

MOSES: Why, in the most simple . . . the most natural way . . . *(Changing his tone)*

Ah! and don't try to trick me either, you clever rascal. If He doesn't address you directly, it's because He doesn't care to. If, on the other hand, He does speak to me, it's because He finds it convenient. Since, at any rate, He's giving the orders, I propose to you that we end this discussion and talk about something else. *(He finishes lacing his sandals. A short time passes.)*

AARON: You can't imagine how disappointing it is not to get answers to questions you ask yourself. Disappointing and exasperating. Listen, just tell me . . .

MOSES: *(Interrupting him)* No! Not another word about it. *(He quickly puts his feet on the floor, making two sharp sounds one behind the other.)* There! Fine shoes for walking. Fine shoes for climbing a steep mountain trail. I believe, all things considered, it's going to turn out extremely well.

AARON: You seem to be in a good mood.

MOSES: I do? Why, I'm in a great mood! Absolutely great! Doing a difficult job, one you know nothing about, not even what it involves, and all that to obey someone you admire . . .

AARON: And fear!

MOSES: And fear . . . for me, that's the beauty of it. Can you understand that?

AARON: I'm trying to.

MOSES: You *must* understand, Aaron. It's the salt of life. If that were not in it . . .

AARON: If that were not in it?

MOSES: For me there would be nothing at all. *(As if talking to himself)* Yes, the salt of life. *(A short time passes.)*

AARON: A sort of . . . slavery, basically.

MOSES: N . . . no, because I can refuse.

AARON: What price would you pay?

MOSES: Don't be thick-headed. He would choose somebody else . . . somebody else, that's all.

AARON: And you would be on pins.

MOSES: I can't hide from you the fact that I would be upset. To be chosen by Him . . . for me that's something . . . monumental . . . so monumental that I place nothing above it.

AARON: So it's a matter of pride then?

MOSES: Maybe, but such pure pride.

AARON: (Interrupting him) No pride is pure! All pride is impure when it leads a man to think that the clay used to fashion him is different from that used to mold his fellow man. For in truth we are all bewildered in the saddest, most heartbreaking equality: the same as ears of corn in a cornfield or grains of sand on a beach. Can you picture a grain of sand getting ready to climb Mt. Sinai? What would the other grains of sand think? (He laughs. Moses laughs too.)

MOSES: (Still laughing) I believe they would think that the mountain-climbing grain of sand is showing them the route to follow. I also believe they would all unite their grains of sand and try to turn their disgustingly flat beach into a majestically imposing mountainside. (Pause. More seriously) Now, if you really want to hear the truth, I'll tell you that as far as I'm concerned, the grains of sand wouldn't think anything, because, to me, they never think.

AARON: Except the mountain-climbing one!

MOSES: Of course, except the mountain climber. Grains of sand are made to be walked on . . . just as ears of corn are grown to be plucked. That's all. Crushed or plucked, take your pick. (A short time passes.)

AARON: You really believe that.

MOSES: Of course. Why?

AARON: I'm just trying to comprehend the reason why you're always in such a hurry to serve as liaison man between the grains of sand and their creator.

MOSES: Aha! Well, I'll tell you . . . it surprises even me. I . . . don't know . . . exactly. It's a deep, compelling force within me radiating toward other people. I sense that they need me, that if I let go of them, only for a fraction of a second, they will fail miserably. I swear to you you couldn't find in that one ounce of pride or even self-glorification. I have pity for them, that's it. They are so feeble, so frightened . . . so quick to go astray —always . . . always, no matter what happens. Have you noticed that when presented with a choice between good and evil, they *always* choose evil, and consistently, without the slightest hesitation?

AARON: Then let go of them. What difference does it make to you whether or not they fail?

MOSES: (After a short pause) Well . . . you see . . . I couldn't let go of them. Something binds us together, something secret, unexplainable.

AARON: Tell me, do you love them?

MOSES: I don't think that's it. If I have any feeling for them, it's no more than a light touch of . . . scorn, yes, that's it, I have a bit of scorn for their weakness, their instability along with their pretentiousness. Ah, that pretentiousness! When you look at them objectively, you feel like giving them a slap in the face, I mean a slap that'll knock their heads off—the hardest slap, the most vengeful slap in the world. But the hard thing, Aaron, is to look at them objectively. There's always something about them which . . . do you know what I mean? . . . which moves you, yes, that's it, something which moves you.

AARON: Yes, I know what you mean.

(Silence. Moses goes slowly to the door; he looks outside.)

MOSES: Day has dawned, but it really is no lighter. It's one of those dreary days that we come across now and then. *(He sighs.)* Well, be that as it may, I've got to get out in it. *(He returns from the door.)*

AARON: Tell me, Moses, what would happen if . . .

MOSES: If what?

AARON: Well, if you, well . . . if you stayed here?

MOSES: What do you mean "here"?

AARON: If you refused to climb those mountain trails in this terrible weather and just stayed here with me?

MOSES: *(Amazed)* Do you know what you're saying?

AARON: Certainly, and it's quite simple. I'm urging you to remain here, under a comfortable shelter, until the weather improves. What could be more natural?

MOSES: Do you think . . . *(He takes a breath.)* One thing astonishes me, you see *(He looks fearfully over his shoulder.)* . . .

the fact that He has not yet felt disposed to manifest His wrath. No doubt, He got the idea I was here for that . . . But, Aaron, think! Once He has given an order, everything has been said; there's nothing else to add, not even a commentary. . . . Remain here? Remain here when He has ordered me to go up on Mt. Sinai?

AARON: All right, forget it. *(Silence. Moses turns round, goes and takes down from the wall a kind of large satchel which he hangs across his shoulder.)*

MOSES: What's in it?

AARON: I don't know for sure, Zipporah filled it. Some cold cuts, I believe, some cheese, a few preserves. Go ahead and look in it. After all, it's for you.

MOSES: *(He half opens the satchel and closes it again immediately.)* No, that holds no interest for me. One does not need to eat so much in order to survive. And as far as something to drink is concerned, there will surely be plenty of springs along the way.

AARON: If they're not frozen over!

MOSES: I'll bet you anything when I get close to them, they'll thaw out.

AARON: Besides, you can always suck the ice, that quenches thirst too.

MOSES: *(Laughing)* Why, of course. Aaron, come now, try not to be unpleasant. I know what you're thinking, and I don't happen to think the same thing, but that doesn't prevent our being compatible brothers, does it? Come, show me that broad smile, and come tell me good-bye. *(Aaron goes near Moses.)*

AARON: *(With emotion)* Moses, good brother, try to take care of yourself. I beg you to be very careful. You can't know how sure, how certain I'd like to be that it's indeed an order from God that you're obeying and not one of those golden dreams which too often carry you away from our world.

MOSES: I give you my word. I'm leaving as I have told you. I haven't concealed a thing from you. Come now, good-bye, Brother. *(He kisses Aaron.)*

AARON: Good-bye, Moses, good-bye. May we soon see each other again.

(Moses walks toward the door, exits, disappears toward the right. A short time passes. He re-enters.)

MOSES: I forgot my staff.

(He takes it from a corner, then exits definitively. Aaron, his head lowered, meditates for a brief moment, then sits down, as in a dream. A short time passes. Nadab, Abihu and Ahisamac, coming from stage left, appear at the door. They hesitate for a few seconds, then enter slowly, one after the other.)

NADAB: *(Whispering, cautiously)* He's gone?

AARON: *(Starts)* Hm? What? Oh, it's you.

NADAB: We just saw him leave.

ABIHU: Yes, we watched him leave, we were careful, you know, very careful, because he doesn't like to be watched.

AARON: There's a whole lot of things he doesn't like.

ABIHU: Yeah. Where's he going?

AARON: What? . . . on the mountain, I suppose . . .

ABIHU: *That,* we know. We saw him take the goat trail, and at a pace you wouldn't believe!

AHISAMAC: If he keeps up that gait, he'll be on top of Sinai before dark.

NADAB: If, of course, that's really his destination.

ABIHU: Yes, if that's *really* his destination. *(Silence)*

NADAB: Well?

AARON: Well, what?

NADAB: We're wondering whether the top of Mt. Sinai is really where he's headed.

AARON: That's what he told me.

ABIHU: He told you nothing else?

AARON: No, just that.

ABIHU: *(Insisting)* And nothing else?

AARON: Nothing else at all.

AHISAMAC: That's not much.

AARON: You know him!

AHISAMAC: Yeah, we know him.

NADAB: And we're even getting to know him well. *(Pause)*

ABIHU: What's he going to do up there? *(Aaron shrugs his shoulders in ignorance.)*

ABIHU: Now don't tell us that he left that part vague too.

AARON: That's what he did, though, and for a good reason: he doesn't know that himself.

NADAB: What did you say?

AARON: He was told only to climb that mountain and to wait up there for his orders.

ABIHU: And you believe that?

AARON: Completely. My brother may be difficult to understand, but he never lies.

AHISAMAC: There're thousands of ways of lying.

AARON: For you, maybe, but not for him.

He always differentiates between . . .

NADAB: *(Interrupting him, impatiently)* . . . Yes, we know, between truth and nontruth, the same as he does between good and evil.

AHISAMAC: As if life were that simple! *(Making a gesture of exasperation)*

AARON: That's precisely what it is for him — a thing of perfect simplicity.

NADAB: A lot of good that'll do him! We're more complicated.

AHISAMAC: Yes. That's what's so very strange . . . even a little shocking about this whole setup — that a very simple man would claim to govern men who are anything but simple.

(The three laugh.)

AARON: Hold on there, just a minute! First of all he doesn't *claim* anything, that's not his style. Next, he does not "govern," he leads, he merely shows the way, and with such carefulness and courtesy that I personally am annoyed. Grown men don't deserve that kind of attention.

NADAB: Don't get upset! Remember we are also careful and courteous. If we weren't . . . *(He stops.)*

AARON: Well? What would happen?

AHISAMAC: Nothing at all, because we *are.*

ABIHU: From the crown of our heads to the soles of our feet. *(Short silence)*

NADAB: Okay, so now what do we do?

AARON: I guess there's only one thing to do: wait till he comes back.

ABIHU: *(Sarcastically)* Great!

AHISAMAC: How long do you think that'll be?

AARON: It's a mystery to me.

AHISAMAC: Not again! What is *not* a mystery in the life of that simple man!

AARON: It's not his fault.

NADAB: Is it ours?

AARON: When he comes round, you get the idea that things tighten up; they become tense. People too. I've noticed that this is always the effect produced by total sincerity on a calculating society. Every little individual stands at a distance, as if to gain enough space for maneuvering. Most of those who speak of my brother do so with bitterness. They cannot believe he is really the way he is. They ask themselves, "What's he hiding?" And that's the mystery.

NADAB: *(A prey to his thoughts)* Total sincerity, you say . . .

AARON: Isn't that what it is?

NADAB: Maybe, but in that case, he's not fit to govern.

AARON: *(Raising his voice)* He's not governing! Do I have to keep telling you that? For that you have your councils, your assemblies, your courts, your factions, your elections. And you harbor inside you an old argumentative spirit which you call political "know-how." That's what's *governing* you. But he . . . *(Changing his tone)* Look, I'll set your minds at ease. I . . . don't understand him. There, that's it. I've said it. I've never understood him. All that he does, or says, always masks that cutting coldness, that chilly abruptness.

NADAB: It's pride.

AARON: Possibly, and I certainly don't see pride as anything nice, but that doesn't keep me from respecting him — or even admiring him. To be what he is so completely! To fill himself until he explodes from it, yes, even to pop the seams of his very being, I find that . . .

NADAB: *(Interrupting him)* Just answer one question for me: do you like him? *(Silence)* Answer me! I'm asking you if you like him.

AARON: *(Hesitating)* Well, he's my brother.

NADAB: There. And that means a kind of abstract attachment forced upon you, but never the enthusiasm of a feeling deep in your heart. Now me, you see, I don't make any bones about it. I don't like him.

ABIHU: Neither do I.

AHISAMAC: Nor I.

AARON: The word is weak: you hate him. You would give a great deal to be relieved . . . rid of him. He bothers you. However discreet he is or tries to be, he takes up too much room. When he's not here, we talk about him, and when we don't talk about him, we think about him.

NADAB: Truthfully now, do you feel that a person like that has a place in a republic? Because I, quite frankly, if others feel as I do, I wouldn't hesitate to banish him.

AARON: Good heavens! Has it come to that?

NADAB: Yes, it has come to that. Don't tell him so!

AARON: Have no fear. I hear all and repeat nothing.

ABIHU: Why, that's it! Banishment. I hadn't thought of that. It's a noble solution —one that won't rock the boat. We certainly

could find a way to mask it under . . . some kind of heading — distant ambassadorship or foreign assignment . . .

AHISAMAC: Say, why not for reasons of health?

AARON: He's as sound as an oak.

AHISAMAC: We can always find a way to *say* it, especially if we are assured of — and this is the beauty of cunning — the complicity of a doctor . . . yes, for example . . . a stay in the country, offered by the State in appreciation for good and loyal services rendered under extremely trying conditions.

AARON: I really pity the one among you who will have to convince him that he's sick.

NADAB: I'll take care of it. I'll manage to whisper in his ear that it's either that or . . .

AARON: Or what?

NADAB: Or retirement. Forever.

AARON: Ah! you would go that far?

NADAB: *(Annoyed)* No, of course not. I didn't mean that. But I *would* go as far as possible. You have no idea how fed up I am with that man.

AARON: You know, it's a good thing for you that I consider myself a kind of impartial referee, and political games leave me cold. Otherwise . . .

NADAB: We have taken you into our confidence. And, you realize, of course, that we could not speak discreetly about certain matters. Emotions take over.

AHISAMAC: No need to beat around the bush. We're all fed up with him. That's all there is to it.

AARON: You didn't always feel that way.

AHISAMAC: Oh, I beg you, Aaron, don't start harping again on how he saved the nation from shame and slavery. That's all ancient history.

AARON: Does that make it less true?

AHISAMAC: Of course, Aaron, of course! The farther it moves away, the less force and substance a memory has.

AARON: Strange theory!

AHISAMAC: Strange, perhaps, but true.

AARON: Very convenient, at any rate, for excusing you from a show of gratitude.

AHISAMAC: Are you kidding?

AARON: I'm becoming wiser.

NADAB: Well, I'll go even farther. And I ask the question sincerely: who knows? Who can know what might have become of the children of Israel if no one had delivered them from Egyptian oppression? Everybody goes around yelling that liberty is the supreme treasure of men and nations. But I wonder whether that's true or not. Maybe it was our lot to live in bondage and to become who we are even beneath the yoke of slavery?

AARON: (With emotion) But, look, Nadab, you know very well . . .

NADAB: Let me finish, please. Just imagine for an instant that our destiny, our true destiny consisted of our fusing, gradually, but intimately, with the Egyptian nation . . . in order to form a third nation, stronger, more powerful than either of the other two. The Egyptian element, for instance, could assure conquests and wage war, while our element could cultivate commerce and amass money. Can you picture that? Do you see what might have come from that? I very sincerely believe that together, we could have been one of the top nations in the world. So from my point of view, what must I think of the man who did not save us, but rather frustrated us by snatching us from Egyptian domination and protection?

AARON: (Shouts) I must be dreaming! What words do you dare utter beneath this roof? What words of sophistry and foolishness? Nadab, we know very well, we know all too well what might have come from that! Egyptian . . . protection lasted long enough for us to see quite well that it made our very existence intolerable. Have you so quickly forgotten your former moaning and groaning? And the sessions held with the Pharaoh by Moses, by me, by others, and maybe even by you, begging him to set us free? All right, granted, we can imagine another path for history, a path other than historical, but only if we look at things clearly, I mean accurately, with a sense of life and reality. I consider it . . . well, unfair, to strike out with one stroke of the pen, for the convenience of a hypothesis, all that we have endured, all that we have . . . suffered under the Pharaohs of Egypt. Take a single example, though an adequate one: the brick proclamation.

ABIHU: What brick proclamation?

AARON: Yes, that's right, you were too young then to remember it, but just ask those two what they think about it.

AHISAMAC: As a matter of fact, that was no laughing matter! (To Nadab) Was it?

NADAB: (After a short pause) No, it really wasn't.

AHISAMAC: It was a rotten time! I can still hear the Pharaoh's taskmasters shouting the orders in the streets and threatening us with their whips. (To Nadab) Do you remember?

NADAB: Only too well! ". . . shall be flogged . . . shall be flogged." It was like a refrain.

AHISAMAC: "Any man who shall not have supplied the quantity decreed by law, shall be flogged with twenty, thirty, fifty lashes." It was horrible!

ABIHU: That's unbelievable! You were flogged? Actually flogged?

AHISAMAC: I'll say we were! And the Pharaoh's whippers, now what were they called?

NADAB: Mastigophores.

AHISAMAC: That's right. And the mastigophores were not at all light-handed! The lashes came down from the sky on our backs like ripe fruit falling from trees in September.

ABIHU: Why, that's insane! Why aren't our children taught this information in school?

AARON: Because . . . you just heard him . . . because "the farther it moves away, the less force and substance a memory has."

ABIHU: That's a good one! I was not flogged — I was too young, but I swear to you, I feel on my back the sting of those whiplashes. (More forcefully) Damn it! I wouldn't have taken that! I couldn't have taken that! I believe, if I had been there, I would have slit the Pharaoh's throat!

NADAB: Talk is cheap!

AHISAMAC: Yes, talk is cheap, but doing it . . . The idea of killing the king of Egypt occurred to thousands of Jews. Only, you know, between the thought and the deed, there is sometimes a vast distance. People think, you see, people think.

ABIHU: Yes, of course, people think. (He sighs.) Why do you call that the brick proclamation?

AARON: Because, precisely, it involved bricks. One day when the Pharaoh was bored, and he was from time to time, he got it in his head that, since he could require anything of us, he would amuse himself by requiring the impossible. Immediately, the order was given to us to make our bricks.

NADAB: We must tell you that we "monopolized" the brickmaking industry in the kingdom of Egypt.

AARON: Yes, to make them without being supplied with the necessary straw.

AHISAMAC: And you definitely need straw to make bricks!

AARON: Up to that time, this straw had been issued to us through the Pharaoh's administrative office. From that day on, though, no more straw!

NADAB: But the same quant ty of bricks.

AHISAMAC: It was up to us to figure our way out of that.

ABIHU: (Indignant) What do you mean "figure" your way out of that?

AHISAMAC: Nobody told us how.

ABIHU: Unbelievable! I find that downright unbelievable. I understand tyranny — at least I can understand it when it's based on something real . . . yes, something difficult, very difficult; but just the same, something possible. But that order to make bricks without straw is odious, because it's impossible — and even ludicrously impossible. You know, I believe you're wrong, I would have indeed slain that fat slob of a pharaoh. I couldn't have restrained myself. If you only knew how my heart is pounding right now! With anger . . . with rage . . and with the disappointment of not having done it. What an unbearable tyrant! *(A long pause)* How was it settled?

AARON Like always. Like a hundred other Pharaonic whims and fantasies were settled. By Moses, thanks to him. *(To the two others who are fidgeting uncomfortably)* Well, is that true or isn't it?

AHISAMAC: *(Regretfully)* It's true.

NADAB: *(Also regretfully)* Yes, it is.

AARON: Moses washed himself, combed his hair . . . he put on his least-worn outfit. Then his long, silent stride took him to the palace of the Pharaoh.

ABIHU: And he received him?

AARON: Yes, oddly enough, the Pharaoh always received him and heard him out. And Moses didn't mince words either. Good Lord, what an outpouring of words! I happened to accompany him two or three times. I was scared to death. I kept saying to myself, "Look out! He's going too far. In two minutes the fine and noble head of your beloved brother will roll across the palace floor." But no such thing happened. Never. I believe Moses fascinated the king of Egypt. The fact remains that, on that occasion, among others, the . . . persecution stopped. And the straw was given back to us. *(Long silence)*

ABIHU: *(A prey to his thoughts)* I . . . didn't know that.

AARON: There are many things you don't know and as a person of influence, you *should* know.

ABIHU: *(Still a prey to his thoughts)* Yes, yes, yes . . . *(Silence again. He goes slowly to the door, and, his back to the audience, leans against the door frame. Then, turning round)* It still doesn't make me like him.

AARON: Nobody is asking you to "like"; you're impossible. You're being asked to respect. It's odd, this mania that all of you have in this country for placing all your human relations on a sentimental plane. I assure you, there are other ways of regarding people. *(Silence. Abihu has turned round toward the outside and looks for a moment without speaking. Suddenly, he gives a start.)*

ABIHU: Say. Did you see that?

AHISAMAC: What? Where?

ABIHU: That fire, on the mountain?

AHISAMAC: On the mountain?

NADAB: A fire?

(They rush to the door. All three look.)

ABIHU: That suddenly caught my eye.

AHISAMAC: No doubt somebody just lit it.

AARON: Nonsense. That fire has been burning since the middle of the night. Moses was here with me when it began.

NADAB: What is it?

AARON: I can't say.

ABIHU: What does Moses say about it?

AARON: He doesn't know what it is either.

NADAB: At last! Something he can't explain.

AARON: We both agreed it's not an ordinary fire.

NADAB: What do you call an ordinary fire?

AARON: A fire made by man for man.

AHISAMAC: Who or what lights a fire that's not for man?

ABIHU: And first, who is it for?

AARON: It's the unavailability of answers to those few questions which makes that fire unusual. Maybe it's like fire from heaven.

NADAB: You mean lightning?

AARON: I mean fire from heaven.

NADAB: Why do you and your brother insist on using ancient ways of speaking? We know very well, nowadays, that it's the storm which produces what you call "fire from heaven."

AARON: Call it lightning or fire from heaven, you hadn't seen this one. You've been here with me half an hour. Not one of you had seen it.

AHISAMAC: We were talking about something else.

ABIHU: And our backs were turned to it.

NADAB: And what's more, we have only your word that it's been burning since midnight. What proof do we have?

AARON: That's the classic example: doubt a truth that's staring you in the face. Nine times out of ten, it works. *(Forcefully)* You have, in fact, my *word* as proof. And since I know that I'm telling the truth, I'm in an excellent position to know that you, Nadab, are insincere. *(More forcefully)* And what's more, you know it too! *(He walks directly in front of Nadab, who backs*

away.) Don't you know it? Sure you do! Look at him squirm! *(Pursuing Nadab)* So admit it! Admit it out loud!

NADAB: *(Confused)* Why? That's ridiculous. Why do you want me to admit that?

AARON: *(Angrily)* Just to have . . . just to see in your mouth, between your lips, something simple, something sincere that we can believe!

NADAB: What do you call "insincere" in the first place?

AARON: It's like counterfeit money that everybody pretends is real in order to use it to pay people off. Our entire society is paid off with that kind of money. Nobody says what he thinks. Nobody thinks about what he does. Nobody does what he wants to. And yet, everybody complains that something is wrong with the world. A colossal wink of the eye makes all men — including me — accomplices in a colossal lie which deceives nobody, but tricks everybody. So that a man who dares tell the truth in this world of trickery immediately appears to be a horrible liar. I'm thinking of Moses, of course. And you three . . . *(Short silence)* Now, then, I ask all of you, and especially you, Nadab, who seem to be the mouthpiece for the others, I ask you to rid yourself of all pretense and frankly answer the question I'm asking you. Why do you dislike my brother?

(Long silence)

NADAB: Because . . . *(He stops.)*

AARON: Go ahead! Because? . . .

NADAB: Because . . . *(Then quickly)* Because he is the way he is. I can't say it any plainer.

54

AARON: All right! And what way is he?

NADAB: I don't know . . . I can't . . . uh . . . express it . . . I already told you: he takes up too much room. I think that's it . . . *(More emotionally)* Wherever you go, you run into him, him or his shadow! Wherever you let your thoughts wander, you suddenly find him there not only ahead of you but whizzing along on his way back while you're still trudging along trying to get there. Moses! Always Moses! It's disconcerting! It's annoying! Do you understand that? He's not of the same caliber as this nation. He's always a bit more lofty. He always has to be a bit more lofty! That's it! Maybe he is a man who could be compatible with the enthusiasm of a young nation, but he definitely is not a man who can appreciate the drudgery of an old nation. That's what I think.

AHISAMAC: So do I.

ABIHU: And I.

NADAB: You understand, it's . . . uh . . . metaphysical. It's unexplainable. There are people like that, now and then, in history or in the streets, a fellow, not particularly outstanding, just a fellow, a regular guy that you come across, and who provokes in you a sudden feeling of aversion, even hostility. And then you say to yourself, "That's strange, can't stand that fellow." Well, I can't stand Moses. That's all. I think this time I've answered you frankly and sincerely.

(Long silence)

AARON: *(As if to himself)* When I think . . . why, when I think that at this very moment, he is no doubt sweating blood and tears on a rough mountain path! And that's hard climbing! . . . and I can see him! I can see him, his head down, his back bent, wet with sweat in spite of the cold weather, and engaging in conversation with himself to forget he's no longer a young man and to forget that he'd be much more comfortable at home by the fire. . . . Then why? Tell me! Why those mountain gymnastics? Because he feels that, in some way or another, his efforts will be beneficial to Israel . . . to the people of Israel. Really, I tell you, it's enough to make you laugh! . . . to make you die laughing! *(He takes a few steps and, stopping suddenly)* Well, gentlemen, that's perfect! I think right now, everything is clear between us, except for a few small feelings I discovered among your secrets, which love the darkness and which my brother would be interested in learning.

NADAB: *(Emotionally)* You won't tell him anything! You promised.

AHISAMAC: Don't forget that: you promised!

ABIHU: Don't go back on your word.

AARON: Have no fear, I'll say nothing. I have no stomach for the job of sneaking myself between the anvil and the hammer. I'll say nothing, I've promised you. But . . . when I suddenly realize how much patience and courage it takes for my brother to be what *he* is among people who are what *you* are, I feel like volunteering as his lieutenant and helping him, with all my might, to accomplish his mission. Take it easy, I'll do nothing. I'm much too lazy to alter the course of my little life, however insignificant it may be. So. With that settled, all has been said. Good night, gentlemen. Or rather, good day, because it's day now. And it's even . . . it will be a fine day, a winter's day, cold and brisk. *(He gently pushes them to the outside.)* Come, you must go home now.

ABIHU: *(As he leaves)* You won't say a word?

AARON: Go on home, I won't say a word.

(They exit. Aaron is left alone on stage.) May this brisk and cold day freely penetrate the home of Moses! May it be at home in the house of Moses, who resembles it and who is as cold, clear, and silent as a fine winter's day.

(He closes the door and walks downstage while the curtain falls.)

ACT II

A slope on Mt. Sinai. Desolate landscape. It is very cold. An intense but flameless fire is burning in the distance, as far away as possible from the audience. Its light is comparable to the glow which precedes the rising sun.

A few seconds after the curtain rises, Moses enters from stage left and comes toward stage right, slowly, deliberately. He begins his climb, and it is difficult. He stops.

MOSES: *(Joyously)* There's the fire again! There it is again . . . burning! I thought I had lost it along the sunken stretch of this path . . . *(He turns his head toward the back of the stage.)* Closer and brighter. *(He takes a few steps toward the fire.)* Greetings to the fire of Mt. Sinai, the fire whose origin nobody comprehends . . . except me . . . and I've guessed its true source. Greetings, fire of the Lord! Fire of God! Fireplace of all heat! Light of lights! From where I stand, still far away from you, I feel your rays even here, and an indescribable feeling of comfort comes over me, goes through me, and that's Faith! *(He shouts.)* I have faith in you! I have faith in you! *(He falls to his knees and bows down to the ground a brief instant. Then getting up again)* You summoned me, I am here. I am ready. Ready to do all it pleases You to command me. Lord, here I am. Here is old Moses, who has been serving You for such a long time and who is ready to serve You still . . . still and always! Give me my orders! You have only to speak. I'm listening . . . I'm listening. . . .

(Pause. It is obvious that he is listening intently, but he makes a quick gesture of disappointment.) I don't hear anything. *(Louder)* I don't hear anything at all. I appeal to the noises on this mountain to stop for a moment. I appeal to that great howling, which must be the wind whistling through the fir trees, I appeal to it to stop. And also to that loud yelping over there *(Pointing)* which is probably the voice of a giddy little fox that has just done something silly. And also to those twittering birds *(Looking up)* that certainly are broadcasting my presence. *(Louder)* I appeal to this

56

mountain; land, water, wind, trees, birds, beasts, all things. I appeal to all things to be quiet around me, that I may hear clearly the voice of God. Quiet, now! Quiet! All of you! That's it there! There, that's better . . . O Lord, Your servant is listening. *(He resumes the position for listening. A rather brief pause, then, in a very ordinary tone of annoyance and impatience.)* Why, that's odd, I don't hear anything. Not a single thing. Come on, come on, Lord, You've got to speak. *(Emotionally)* I'm here. I'm waiting. My ear is wide open — like a hungry mouth. Feed it! It's Your job to feed it. *(Pause)* No? Still nothing? *(He yells.)* Well, what's going on? *(Silence. Completely at a loss, he wanders about for a minute, to the right and to the left of the stage, then he comes downstage and sits down on a large rock.)* And yet, Lord, yet . . . You did summon me. Didn't You? It was You who summoned me? . . . Or else . . . or else . . .

(Panic-stricken, he leaps to his feet. He takes a few confused steps backward, with nervous agitation, then returning to his seat) Or else, this is going to be like the other times. It will be necessary, it will still be necessary for me to figure this out . . . to untangle all this in order to distinguish fact from fiction . . . in order to separate divine orders from the human babble that drowns them out, in order to extract the orders from the noise! I'll do it too, like I've always done it. Only, Lord, only, keep in mind: this is a job for a young man . . . one who is afraid of nothing . . . neither a simple mistake nor a serious delusion; neither the wrong path nor the straight and narrow. This is a job for

a man thirty or thirty-five years old. But at my age, Lord! Do You truly believe that I can be the man needed by You? The man needed by these people who are disgruntled? Quarrelsome? Stubborn and so fickle? You see . . . you see . . . even on the verge of starting out, I feel . . . I don't know . . . a kind of heavy weariness—binding . . . paralyzing my hands and feet. I feel as though I have no more muscles, no more bones . . . as though I'm made solely of soft, vanishing flesh. Hear me, I think . . . I sincerely think Your servant is coming to the end of his line, and You're soon going to have to find someone to replace him, someone who . . . *(He interrupts himself, gets up suddenly. Forcefully)* Lord! I sense so clearly what should be, *the one* who should be the man to succeed me . . . that ardor, that energy, that kind of passion he should have and I remember having myself long ago. Always ready, never weary . . . tireless! And good-natured, yes, especially that — unchangingly good-natured. I've been criticized for being grouchy. They say . . . they say I'm a kind of bear — and the worst kind. They say when I happen to smile, it's only after I have practiced that smile for a long time in front of my mirror, and the slightest obstacle I meet, the slightest blunder I make, causes it to vanish so that I'm once again growling, frowning, and to tell the truth, rather ugly. Maybe they're right, I don't know, I don't know anymore. I am the way I am, and the folks these days don't like that. It's a sign of growing old, the world moves farther and farther away from you, until you are left alone, all alone in a cemetery where your contemporaries are no more than eroding dates on tombstones. And the wind over this desert which surrounds you, the wind of loneliness, which whispers all alone, like an old dotard, muttering, mumbling out stories from another time, that nobody even cares to hear anymore . . . Getting old, Lord, getting old! You don't know what that is, You're eternally young, like the Rock of Gibraltar. You who remain the same when all else changes, when all else passes on around You. But me, I know. Sure I do, I know what old age is. I have seen it, I have felt it coming to me day after day . . . descending on me, flowing slowly into me, like a lazy serpent settling down to hibernate. So, now . . . *(He stops short and turns abruptly toward the back of the stage.)* Wait a minute! I just felt . . . Aha! I distinctly felt something like a bolt of lightning flashing deep down inside me . . . the lightning of certainty, a sort of light which permeates and illuminates the depths of your soul . . . much brighter and clearer than the gentle . . . tender light of faith: I know . . . that's it, I know. *(He advances upstage. With a certain solemnity)* I know that You *are* in that fire . . . that You are concealed . . . that You are hidden in that fire on the mountain. I know. I suddenly realized that if You don't manifest Your presence more clearly, it's because You've got Your reasons, and that all I have to do is bow before them . . . which I now do, Lord, with respect, with confidence, and, if You allow me, with child-like devotion. I bow. *(He bows toward the fire.)* I bow. *(He suddenly turns around and bows toward the audience.)* I bow before You, but, but *where* are You? *(He puts his hand to his ear, listening.)* Where *are* You? That's strange. I can't spot the exact direction . . . or the origin of Your voice. It seems to be in everything . . . it seems to be everywhere. Where's it coming from . . . just where's it coming from . . . *(He runs all across the stage, with mounting excitement.)* . . . this voice of the Creator? The powerful voice of the Creator of all things? This voice that, all at once, reverberates within me, rises up from the deepest recesses of my being. What am I saying, "reverberates?" Resounds, yes, thunders! Yes, it thunders! It explodes! I am completely under its spell . . . completely possessed by this voice which commands . . . this overwhelming voice which suddenly is beginning to dictate its will to me . . . *(He stops abruptly, frozen in his tracks; one guesses that he is listening intently.)* Yes, Lord . . . yes, Lord, I'll obey . . . *(One should feel that this is the audible half of the dialogue; the other half, the divine half, is naturally inaudible to the audience.)* But, I beg You, don't go too fast! Don't go too fast, give me . . . time . . . time . . . But where? I ask You, where can I look for that? Where can I find that? . . . I understand, Lord, I understand very well, don't get impatient, I'll manage, I'll work it out . . . *(He yells.)* No! Don't be discouraged, it'll work, You'll see, it'll work! I know, yes, I realize it's a little . . . humiliating, in Your omnipotence, a little . . . uh . . . degrading to have to call on an old man, to have to use as intermediary a feeble old man, almost an invalid, but that's how it is, what can I do? That's how it is. I guess we'll have to do the best we can, You and I . . . Hm? What did You say? What did You just say? . . . I didn't get the end of the sentence. Excuse my ears. Forgive them for being so old and for confusing half the words. But why, tell me, why are You talking so fast? That's right! Why are You spitting the words out like that? Take Your time, come on! That's it, there, that's better. Now, wait. Wait a second. Let me find, let me make something to write on. Can You suggest something? I wasn't expecting that, believe me! Otherwise I would have brought along paper and pencil . . . *(Quickly)* for the rough draft, of course, for the rough draft! Later, I would have copied it over with a pen, a fine golden pen, on parchment . . . Of course, of course. Why do You talk to me as though I were an uninformed child? I know everything, that's right, absolutely everything about all that is due You and I'm ready . . . *(He stops.)* Yes, yes, I'm sorry! I always stray from the subject, and I embellish things, and chatter and prattle like an old woman. The fact is I'm, You have to understand me, I'm completely dumfounded by the honor that You do me by even speaking to me. It has been going on for more than forty years now, and I still am not used to it. But it'll be all right if, if . . . You'll see! *(Assuming a different tone)* Good! I'll cut out the flowery language, just the essential. But before anything else, something to write on, that's what I've got to find; on what can I worthily reproduce the divine word of God? . . . Let's see . . . Let's see . . . *(He*

goes slowly across the stage searching diligently for something appropriate.) . . . A rock? Why not? A fine, flat piece of rock left behind on this rock-covered mountain from the beginning of time by the mighty, creative hand of God? Let's find a rock . . . This one? No, too narrow . . . That one over there? No, too lumpy. Something vast, wide, like the Lord Himself . . . Aha! this time . . . *(He stoops behind a boulder.)* I think I've got it! *(He stands up with a stone tablet in his hands.)* This is the tablet that God desires . . . the tablet for the divine law. *(He yells.)* Lord! I've got it. I found it. Go ahead, You can dictate now. Just give me time to pick up a piece of chalk . . . here's one, there . . . good! That's it. Let's get started! *(A short time passes.)* Hey, there, not so fast . . . And how should I write that down? Word for word? Or should I paraphrase? I mean, do You want me to summarize? . . . *(A short period of silence during which his face expresses amazement. His voice rising)* What? What? What? Should I take *that* down? Hm? Take it easy, Lord. Don't yell so loud! . . . *(A long period of silence, then, under his breath, as in an aside)* Oh! Good heavens, what a deafening noise! What's the matter with Him? Just listen to that racket! I don't know what just made Him mad, but you can believe He's furious right now . . . Go ahead then! Go on! Just listen to Him let go . . . I hope I'm not the one who upset Him. Seriously, I ask you. *(To the audience)* Hm? It couldn't be because of me. You saw it, I have been careful and respectful . . . unless . . . unless . . . I may have uttered, unawares, a word or two that may have been a bit too harsh? At any rate, I don't remember it. *(He breathes.)* You see . . . you see . . . how upsetting it is dealing with Him. *(Correcting himself quickly)* No, no, not upsetting, just . . . uh . . . difficult. That's it — difficult. I mean simply that my relationship, that *the* relationship between a man and his creator, well, it's not all milk and honey . . . ah, there! He's calming down. He's speaking more slowly. He says . . . *(He listens.)* Now wait a minute . . . sure, that's right . . . that's absolutely right . . . He's asking — and full of wrath! — what good there is in giving laws to a group of people who break them beforehand, ten times a day. And that's a question that I have even asked myself very often. You'd think that laws were made for people to challenge them . . . and scoff at them . . . *(Listening)* Why, of course . . . of course . . . that's exactly right. *(To the audience)* He says that more and more He has the feeling that the world is making fun of Him. The world! Just think about that for a minute. After all, He's the one who made it; errors excepted, of course, errors excepted! *(He laughs to himself. Then changing his tone)* Ah! that I didn't know, I didn't know at all . . . *(To the audience)* Say, it seems that last night there was another frontier incident in . . . now where was that? Let me think . . . in Gaza, on the Gaza side. It was there that a group of Israelis met a party of Egyptians and, of course, they lit into each other like wildcats. Result: seven dead and . . . I don't know how many wounded. Discouraging, very discouraging! *(A short time passes.)* And that's what makes Him angry; that's what makes Him furious. I was sure it couldn't have been me. Seven dead, say now, without counting the wounded, who are sure to die of their wounds, that's a terrible picture . . . a terrible picture of the hunt . . . and I understand . . . No, wait! He says that when He has received the reports from Syria, Iran, Lebanon, and other Arab regions, He will total them all up, and it will be, once again . . . wait! . . . what? Discouraging. Did you notice that? He used the same word I did. And there He goes clearing out of here — getting back on His great steeds. And I understand Him. *(Getting enthusiastic)* And I understand Him! It's a fact! Really! What kind of cutthroats are those people to divide the world between their two camps? Who dreamed up this horde of assassins? This gang of murderers? For an aye or a nay, everybody kills everybody else, and the killers are always right. Justice, misunderstood; patriotism, misunderstood; courage, bravery, spirit of sacrifice, all that misunderstood, and as a result the assassins are transformed into heroes. So that's it, you see, He can't stand it anymore. And I can't either. There! *(He yells.)* I can't either! He says . . . we say, those murders were perhaps permissible in the past, when man had nothing to call his own, except — and that's true today too — his person, and everything outside his person could be taken as the enemy. But now! But today! When we should have only friends around us, and two minutes of conversation, less than that, a handshake, even less, a simple, friendly wink should suffice to . . . *(He interrupts himself.)* Wait! Wait! Here's the report from Jordan. *(A short time passes; he listens.)* Of course! What did I tell you! At the Israeli-Jordanian border . . . confrontation between an Israeli troop and a Jordanian patrol—patrol! How about that! Two dead and nine wounded. That's it. Round two. And who started it? That's the mystery. Was it him? No, not at all—he's the one! I swear it . . . I give you my word, and I'm willing to fight to prove my point. Child's play, all of it! Deadly child's play, but child's play nonetheless. Now it may be, Ladies and Gentlemen of Israel and elsewhere, it may be that you are mature and do not have the right to play the child. Murder is a strictly forbidden thing. There. No killing! . . . Yes, Lord, I've got it, and I'll explain it to them — no killing, no matter what the pretext may be. How do You want me to write that down? How do You say that in Your language? Ah! All right. Thou? . . . Thou shalt not kill. Excellent! Wait, let me write that in big, tall letters . . . *(He writes.)* Thou . . . shalt . . . not . . . kill . . . Good! I couldn't have said it better. Thou shalt not kill. All right. Not for this reason, nor for that reason, nor for any other reason . . . Not at all! Period! Now *that's* talking. And the first one who kills, I condemn him, we condemn him to death . . . death by stoning, and you can believe that's not funny; stones for paving, as big as that *(He gesticulates.)* which hit you square in the face! Makes you wish you were somewhere else. Good! It's said.

Let's move on . . . But first, You must realize that if man, all at once, were denied the pleasure of killing . . . the pleasure and profit, the pleasure, the profit, and the convenience of killing his fellow man, the air that we breathe here, I mean on earth, would suddenly become completely breathable again, perfectly breathable, and there would no longer be the need to go to the moon in search of other battlefields for waging other wars. Good!

On that note, Lord, please give me the second law! The second commandment of the divine code. I'm listening. With the total attention of my old ears, I'm listening to Your great voice. *(He places his fingers around his ear and leans forward attentively as the curtain slowly falls.)*

ACT III

A meeting room, where about twenty notables are assembled. They are talking to each other, thereby producing a muffled murmuring, from which arises all at once, a line from a particular conversation. In the upstage left corner of the room there is a small dais on which Nadab, who is chairing the meeting, sits chatting with an attendant standing near him.
When the curtain rises, the general murmuring demands the attention of the audience. A short time passes. Nadab arises.

NADAB: *(In a loud voice)* Gentlemen, I beg you, a little silence! It sounds as though we're at the market on Saturday afternoon.

RUBEN: It's just that we have so much to say to one another.

MANASSEH: We haven't held a meeting in weeks. We've got to talk to each other.

NADAB: Then talk softly!

SIMEON: *(Impetuously)* Impossible! When I have something to say, it has to come out.

NADAB: Well, for the moment, hold it in! It'll come out later. *(General laughter, then rising murmur)*

APPARITOR: Silence, gentlemen, please! *(The murmuring is reduced by half.)* Announcing Jigal, the son of Joseph, of the tribe of Issachar. *(Jigal enters, shakes a few hands, then disappears in the crowd.)* And Hosea, the son of Nun, of the tribe of Ephraim. Here is Hosea. *(Hosea enters as did Jigal and gets settled.)*

SODI: Well? May we begin?

NADAB: No, Caleb, Gaddi and Guenel aren't here yet.

SODI: Listen, Nadab, this is too much. There'll always be some slowpokes. The rest of us were here on time. They only had to do as we did.

SIMEON: There's surely someone else who's absent — Aaron. He's the one I'm interested in.

RUBEN: I wonder just what he'll be able to say.

MANASSEH: I wouldn't want to be in his shoes.

SIMEON: Oh, you know Aaron never has trouble finding something to say.

APPARITOR: Announcing Guenel, son of Maki, of the tribe of Gad. *(Guenel enters.)*

NADAB: You're late, Guenel.

GUENEL: Yes, you'll excuse me, I hope. My wife went out, and there was no one to keep an eye on the shop.

NADAB: Don't worry, it's all right.

APPARITOR: Announcing Caleb, son of Jephunneh, of the tribe of Judah. *(Caleb enters.)*

CALEB: *(Looking a bit sheepish)* Greetings, everybody. Don't tell me I'm late, I know it only too well. All my life I've always been late.

NADAB: Maybe fate has so decreed it.

CALEB: You're joking, but I've been telling myself that for a long time! *(General laughter, then resumption of the murmurs and the individual conversations.)*

SODI: *(To Dan)* As for me, the thing I dislike about Moses is his way of always confronting you with the accomplished fact. I can't stand that.

DAN: You're right, neither can I.

SODI: Politics, my good fellow, thrives on group activity, in an assembly, after long and sometimes heated debates. We vote, and the majority rules. Nothing more simple or more just.

DAN: Yes, except when the majority of those assembled are imbeciles.

SODI: That can't happen.

DAN: Hmph!

SODI: No, that can't happen. You forget

that the members of the assembly are elected by universal suffrage.

DAN: So what? Do you think the fact of having the right to vote confers upon you a degree in intelligence? *(He bursts out laughing.)* Don't get upset, you can see I'm only teasing you.

SODI: Ah! Good. I was afraid! *(He laughs also, then seriously)* You know, I just can't stand that guy creating his politics all by himself, without accepting any advice. When I see him plotting his decisions in secret and then proclaiming, "This is what I have decided. Bow down and obey!", I feel like doing I don't know what.

DAN: I'm like you, Sodi, I find that . . . humiliating. Yes, that's the best way to describe it: I feel humiliated.

APPARITOR: Announcing Gaddi, son of Susi, of the tribe of Joseph. *(Gaddi enters.)*

ALL: *(Acknowledging his arrival jokingly)* Ah!

MANASSEH: *(Laughing)* That's the last of the flock.

GADDI: And I almost didn't make it. My wife was against it.

NADAB: What do you mean "against it"? Is your wife the boss of your house?

GADDI: N-no, of course not. You see I wound up here after all, don't you? But it wasn't easy. My wife fears nothing, and she has a way of choosing words . . . She didn't want me to come waste my time, here, with you. Waste my time, how about that! You have to realize she's definitely pro-Moses.

SIMEON: *(Yells)* Female followers, that's all he's got now.

RUBEN: Female followers! Come now! I'm convinced that my wife is more enraged against him than I am.

SODI: So is mine. I could tell you . . .

NADAB: Let's not start telling things.

MANASSEH: Say, Gaddi, family life must not be so hot at your house, hm?

GADDI: We finally worked things out, but it wasn't at all easy. There are still some matters that we never bring up. For example . . .

NADAB: *(Yelling)* Didn't you hear me? Enough about that. *(All become silent.)* Good! We're all here . . .

GADDI: Except Aaron!

NADAB: Except Aaron, but he'll be here later, he gave me his word. I think we can begin.

APPARITOR: Quiet, everybody! We're about to begin. *(Complete silence)*

NADAB: Now, you all know why we are assembled. It's about Moses . . . *(A general booing interrupts him.)*

VARIOUS SHOUTS: Boo! Boo! Enough! Out with him! Run him off! String him up! *(Et cetera)*

APPARITOR: Silence!

NADAB: If we begin like that, we'll be here until tomorrow . . . at least! Now, gentlemen, whatever your opinion may be of the man and of his actions, I assure you that it *is* possible to speak calmly about it. What's more, if you refuse to do so, someone else can preside over this meeting, and I'll go back home. Is that understood? *(Silence)* All right. The questions which you will have to answer are quite easy and hardly merit a passionate response. Here's the first. It has been three weeks today since Moses left.

MANASSEH: Three weeks and two days!

NADAB: *(Furious)* Don't interrupt me with such foolishness!

MANASSEH: I wasn't interrupting you, I was supporting you.

NADAB: Support me with your silence. *(Continuing)* As I was saying . . . ah, yes, it's a matter of finding out what you believe has become of Moses during this long absence. Is he dead, do you suppose, or alive? Vanished? Or what else? That's the first question.

RUBEN: "Vanished," how? What do you mean?

NADAB: Eh! I don't know a thing about it. You know him as well as I do. He likes sensational developments, disappearances, suspense in other words. You might say that his life with us has been no more than a long series of conjuring tricks. From the plagues in Egypt to the crossing of the Red Sea, nothing but magic tricks. Remember how fond the Pharaoh was of them . . .

RUBEN: I wouldn't swear that he relished the last one so much.

NADAB: *(Laughing)* He surely must have found the Red Sea a bit too salty! *(General laughter, then silence.)*

MANASSEH: All right. So what's the point?

NADAB: I don't know, I tell you. I'm just like you, I'm trying. Just suppose, I don't know . . . that he is spending some time there . . . and that he'll suddenly return, surprising everybody, in that theatrical style in which he is a consummate artist. *(A short time passes.)*

MANASSEH: *(Naively)* Return to do what?

NADAB: How should I know? You surprise me! To . . . make us accept, with that reverence that people show to those who return from distant countries . . . to make us willingly swallow, with our eyes closed, for example . . . ever so slight a change in the constitution . . . or at least, something of that nature. *(A short time passes. Everybody ponders what has just been said.)*

SODI: *(Flaring up)* We know nothing! I was just telling Dan a minute ago, we never know anything! With that old fox, everything is cloaked in mystery. When did he leave? How could he survive? Did he take along supplies? And how many? Heavy clothes to brave the cold winds? Blankets? Weapons? What? What? Now, you know, climbing Sinai all alone, this time of year, is not just a pleasant little hike!

ABIHU: No, it's not! The three of us here tried to get to the bottom of this wild escapade: Nadab, Ahisamac and I. All three of us went to his residence on the day, the very hour of his departure. We hid. We watched him leave. We saw him set out, with a hearty stride, I must say, on a mountain path. Afterwards, we went to the tent of his brother Aaron.

GADDI: It's true, we still have *him*! What's he up to?

NADAB: He was supposed to come a bit later, and yet, not this late. Go on, Abihu.

ABIHU: Well, we spoke for a long time with his brother, but he could tell us nothing, for he knew nothing.

GADDI: *(Sneering)* Naturally!

ABIHU: No, it's not what you think. He *really* didn't know anything. Moses had told him nothing. Maybe it's odd, but that's the way it is. In addition, we got the impression, didn't we, Nadab, that Aaron would probably be with us.

SODI: *(Still angrily)* Go against his own brother! Still it's not unheard of. What do you think? Is he crazy . . . maybe?

NADAB: Aaron? Come now! I've never met a more stable person. To such an extent that I'd say not one of you is as stable as he is.

MANASSEH: That remains to be seen!

NADAB: It's already seen — a will of iron, with splendid brains. That's why I've called you together, to get a feeling of unity and to obtain a decision from the group . . . perhaps unanimous, without trying to influence you . . . which brings me back to the question: what has become of Moses during these three long weeks?

SIMEON *(Ill-tempered)* How do you expect us to know?

NADAB: It's not a question of knowing. I'm merely asking for your feelings about the matter, the ideas you have about it. Now I, for example, I believe he's dead. *(A short time passes.)*

RUBEN: And what if he's alive? And hiding, as you said, before reappearing?

NADAB: That's my second question. Then, what shall we do about it? How shall we behave toward him? *(A short time passes, then as a quick discovery.)*

SIMEON: Well, we forget about him.

That's it! We forget about him, quite simply, and we go on to something else, as if he weren't here, as if he'd never been here.

NADAB: *(Thinking)* All right . . . yes . . . I think I see . . . *(Continuing)* So that dead or alive, our attitude is the same — total indifference?

SIMEON: That's right!

VOICES: Yes, yes, that's right! Very good! Good idea! That seems right!

SIMEON: And that doesn't complicate life. "Moses? Don't know him." And I go about my business, whether he likes it or not. *(General acquiescence)*

VOICES: Bravo! That's what we'll do. That's what we must do!

(Aaron suddenly enters from upstage, very excited.)

AARON: *(Yelling)* Come now, Nadab, come now! I can't believe I'm hearing this. Don't allow them to say such stupid things! *(He makes his way to the dais and faces the others. He takes a brief instant to catch his breath and to regain his composure.)* I'll tell you my feelings immediately, that will simplify our relationship. I believe my poor brother is dead. If he were not, I don't see how he could subject me to such anguish. During his previous absences, he has always managed to send me . . . a word, a message. On the other hand, whatever the thing was . . . the business which led him to climb Sinai, I find it difficult to believe that it may have taken more than three weeks to accomplish. So, alas, he's dead. And I hope with all my heart that he died without suffering, regret or bitterness of any kind . . . *(More sharply)* Now, if perchance, he were alive and came back some day to live among his people, don't imagine for one minute that you could act, in his presence, as if he were not there. *(More forcefully)* Indifference? Don't make me laugh. Total indifference? That's it, you see, it's that word which dug into me and made me charge through that door behind which I was awaiting the end of your deliberation. That's the thing that infuriated me. *(Even more forcefully)* But how? Yes, how do you manage to be what you are? How do you arrange your lives so as never to make any progress? To remain always petty, careful, fearful, greedy, cruel, cowardly, cowardly . . . *(Insistent general protests; he yells.)* . . . cowardly! *(Silence)* Of three or four solutions, you always choose instinctively the most small-minded, the least dangerous for you, the most damaging for the other person. Act as if he weren't here! The very idea! Why, my good friends, it wouldn't take him five minutes to convince you that he is here. With a single glance — only one — he would silence you and stop you right in your tracks. And all of you would gather around him as a collective individual to ask him imploringly what you could do to please him. That's the way you are! *(More softly)* That's the way you are. I assure you that your meeting, when stripped of all non-essentials, and heard from the other side of that door where I was, free from the heat and press of the crowd . . . your meeting made a . . . pitiful impression on me out there. *(He sighs.)* All at once, I got the impression that you were sick, seriously sick. There, I've said what I had to say.

(He starts to come down from the dais.)

NADAB: Wait! Wait! *(Deferentially)* This sickness . . . how would you treat it? And can it be treated? Have you thought about that?

AARON: Me? Frankly, no. On my word, I joined you here with the sole intention of strengthening your ranks and, in turn, giving my opinion, just like everybody else. But when I heard, just before I came in, I don't know who yelling out advice about forgetting my brother, or acting in his presence as if he were dead, and everybody's voice rising in a chorus of agreement, oh, I must confess it, my blood boiled. *(He becomes more emotional.)* Forget! Do you realize what you're saying? Forget! To treat a man already here — or who just appeared — as if he no longer existed, as if he didn't exist, as if he had left no trace, not even a footprint, or a fingernail, of his presence on earth. Just think now that this man, this outcast, the man we . . . you're about to delete, you're planning to delete is . . . Moses! The great, the one and only, the real Moses — deleted, yes, by a bunch of . . . of . . .

NADAB: Easy, Aaron, calm down!

AARON: Yes, yes, you're right. Those who don't know me well could imagine that I push family ties to . . . but you know it's not so. I derive no satisfaction from being the brother of a great man; it's a situation I have always considered as being one of the most awkward. I'll go even further. In my brother, in his nature, in his life, in his way of being and acting, there are some things with which I disagree.

NADAB: What, for example?

AARON: Well, why . . . *(He interrupts himself. Changing his tone)* No, that would take too long. I can only tell you that as far as relations with others are concerned, if I were Moses, I would seek to make them a little easier, yes, a bit more cheerful. I'd strive to reduce the coldness . . . the haughtiness of my behavior with others. *(He comes down from the dais.)*

SODI: Ah! But just the same! You're saying exactly what I said, Aaron.

AARON: But not the way you said it, with that sneer, that grumbling, that tone of objection . . . of vengefulness. *(He crosses the room and stops in front of Sodi.)* My brother is not the director of the department for public complaints. Moses . . . is Moses, totally in and of himself, and totally himself. Accept him or reject him, but do so totally.

VOICES: We reject! Yes! We reject! We all reject him!

AARON: *(Wearily)* Well, reject him then. Even he would be furious if he could see me defending him. *(Long silence)*

NADAB: *(Gently)* Try to understand, Aaron. What is happening before your eyes and mine — for I insist on saying it — has not been previously planned by us to produce this demonstration. Yes, what is happening here today has been growing slowly, building up pressure for a long time. Suddenly it explodes. Why, do you suppose? Because as soon as it became too strong in each of us individually, this tension was determined to overpower us collectively. Our different grievances, which were tolerable so long as they were private, became unbearable when exposed to the group. And so, everything explodes.

AARON: Oh, I had no doubt about that.

NADAB: Maybe your brother has — this is merely a hypothesis — lived beyond the time, shorter than we imagine, when a man is followed, heeded, or admired by other men. It's possible, I don't know. At any rate, I assure you, in all that occurred today before you there was nothing . . . degrading . . . either to Moses or to us . . .

AARON: Except certain expressions which I found, I must say, vulgar or insulting.

NADAB: Of course, but you know as well as I that a great step will be taken in human friendship the day we find a way to suppress verbal violence. But that's easier said than done.

All right. The thing we need to know now is whether in the battle that we wage for our freedom, you, Aaron, are with us, against us, or simply neutral. *(A short time passes.)*

AARON: Before responding to the substance of the question, I must tell you that I abhor, even loathe, certain ways of talking, borrowed, if I may say so, from the rhetoric of politicians. For example, just what is this *battle* that you're waging? For *your* freedom. Could you seriously maintain that my brother is a threat to that freedom?

NADAB: As you say, Aaron, it's a way of talking — expressing oneself.

AARON: I don't like it.

NADAB: All right.

AARON: I don't like it at all.

NADAB: We'll avoid it. Let's leave it for

the time being. As far as the rest is concerned, what do you say?

AARON: Well, now, the innate indolence of a lymphatic nature would lead me, in a sly manner, to declare myself neutral. However, overcoming my nature, I'll tell you that, basically, I don't see why, supposing my brother dead, I would not lend support, even with an indulgent smile on my face, to the efforts that you will make to govern yourselves. I warn you: it will be difficult.

NADAB: No one knows that better than I. A whole world to recreate. Other laws, other customs and especially — and especially another way of thinking. We decided something in the conversations we held prior to this meeting. We . . . we decided to choose a kind of . . . patron of our new life . . . a kind of guide for our existence . . .

AARON: But you had Moses!

NADAB: Yes, but for all practical purposes, we don't have him anymore. Imagine, Aaron, imagine the effigy, the statue of this patron, of this fellow worker, placed right in the middle of the room where we are! Can you see that?

AARON: Not very well. Nothing, I hope, resembling a deity?

NADAB: No, absolutely not. The idea would not occur to any of us to offer, shall I say, disloyal competition to the God of Moses.

AARON: What do you mean, the God of Moses! Yours too, I hope.

NADAB: Ours, of course, ours. No, a mere . . . symbol. That's the word I want. A symbol of our daily work.

AARON: Let's carry it a bit further. What symbol?

NADAB: Well, a sort of . . . animal, that's it, a domestic animal, that we would make of gold, to render it more precious, and on which we would keep our eyes fixed in order to recall how much our life has changed, how we must direct it ourselves by tilling the soil and raising animals. You see?

AARON: I see. At least I think I do. What sort of animal?

NADAB: Oh, I don't know, it makes no difference. A horse, a cow, a bull, a humble companion of our daily labor, suddenly . . . well . . . honored. Wouldn't that be beautiful?

VOICES: Yes, yes. Superb! Magnificent! (Applause)

AARON: If you are wealthy enough to afford a bull molded of gold, then somebody is mistaken about the proverbial poverty of Israel.

NADAB: But, Aaron, listen. We don't have that gold, or rather we have it in pieces, in little fragments. It was felt that each of us could contribute his jewels: rings, necklaces, earrings . . .

AARON: It would take jewels galore to make a golden bull!

NADAB: We're not insisting on the bull. If you think the bull is too big, let's choose his son, then, so to speak . . . for example, take the calf.

AARON: (Thinking) A golden calf.

NADAB: Yes, a golden calf that we would place in the middle of this room and which would be present at all our sessions.

AARON: *(Still thinking)* A calf . . . fashioned of gold, I find that childish.

NADAB: So do I, but what of it? It's only a symbol

AARON: A childish symbol.

NADAB: But, Aaron, a symbol, whatever it is, is always childish, just as it is childish to try to express something immense by using something scanty.

AARON: Or vice versa.

NADAB: Or vice versa. *(To the others)* Well, shall we do it?

VOICES: Yes, yes, we'll do it! Hurrah! The golden calf! The golden calf!

NADAB: All of you will come, in single file, to this dais and deposit your rings and other items of gold jewelry. Afterwards, we shall leave this room and return to our homes to get the rest from our wives.

GADDI: Uh, Uh! Mine is going to put up an awful fuss!

NADAB: All right now! Let's get started.

APPARITOR: Come forward one by one. Slowly! And orderly! Put your gifts on this table. Come, gentlemen, come forward. Come on, Shammna! *(Shammna comes forward. He removes a ring from his finger and puts it down as instructed.)* Shammna, son of Zaccur, tribe of Ruben. One gold ring. Next, come, gentlemen. *(Shapbath comes forward. Same procedure)* Shapbath, son of Hori, tribe of Simeon, one gold ring. *(Caleb comes forward. Same procedure)* Caleb . . .

NADAB: Well, for once, Caleb is not late.

(To Caleb) You see, there's hope.

APPARITOR: Caleb, son of Jephunneh, tribe of Judah. One gold ring. Come! Move forward! *(Palthi comes forward.)* Palthi, son of Raphu, tribe of Benjamin, one . . . excuse me, two gold rings.

NADAB: Good, Palthi. You do things in a grand manner.

PALTHI: *(Very deliberately)* I always do my best.

NADAB: *(Smiling)* One has only to look at you to be convinced.

(Gaddiel comes forward.)

APPARITOR: Gaddiel, son of Sodi, tribe of Zebulon, one gold ring. *(Gaddi approaches.)* Gaddi, son of Susi, tribe of Manasseh. One gold ring.

NADAB: Say, Gaddi, you're not giving your earring?

GADDI: Not on your life! Do you want my wife to tear me to pieces? If you only knew how she's going to squawk when she discovers this ring missing from my finger. And she'll notice it immediately. *(He exits and repeats.)* She'll notice it immediately. *(Laughter)*

APPARITOR: Come now, let's keep moving! *(Sethur comes forward.)* Sethur, son of Michael, tribe of Asher. One gold ring. *(Nachbi comes forward.)* Nachbi, son of Vephsi, tribe of Naphtali . . .

AARON: *(In the foreground, alone)* A golden calf . . . the golden calf. It's strange, there's something about it I like . . .

(The curtain falls slowly.)

ACT IV

On Sinai.

As the curtain rises, Moses is seen walking hurriedly across the stage. A long time passes. Suddenly, he stops and, looking toward the sky:

MOSES: *(Exasperated)* But after all . . . how? How does it happen that I no longer get an answer? Hm? Never any answer anymore? What's the matter? What's going on? *(He resumes his walking, then stops abruptly once again.)* It's been three weeks . . . what am I saying! *(He counts mentally.)* It's been *more* than three weeks since I came up here. What patience I've had! *(Rapidly, toward the sky)* And You, too, all right! *(To the audience, as if confidentially)* It's true that it took the patience of Job for me to get from Him, bit by bit, this confounded . . . this confounded . . . what does He call it? Oh, yes — a decalogue. *The* decalogue! Funny name, because *deka,* if I'm not mistaken, means ten — ten laws, ten commandments. Yes, but the annoying thing, you see, is that according to the way I counted them the day before yesterday, there were already twelve . . . or maybe even thirteen . . . and all that . . . enclosed in a pile of observations, remarks, appendices — about the altar, about holocausts . . . about the oil . . . about the brass basin . . . about perfumes or meats . . . in short, I'm getting lost in it. *(He throws his head back and yells toward the sky.)* I'm getting lost in it! There! *(He comes downstage, sits pouting and thinks for a brief instant. Suddenly to the audience)* When one is the Lord, one is supposed to know what he wants. *(Forcefully)* And one is supposed to express it! Precisely, without any frills or curlicues or fancy, evasive language. Yes, one must state his will clearly, realizing that the poor mortal who receives this in his ear is precisely just a poor mortal who perhaps did not invent clay. You recognize in this portrait the spit and image of me. *(He sighs, gets up, takes a few nervous steps, then comes to sit down again.)* Everybody today talks about dialogue — that of God with man, no matter how little man contributes to this . . . exchange . . . an exchange . . . that's it, a free and peaceful exchange, that's how I see things. *(A short time passes.)* Only, it takes at least two to have a dialogue, and most of the time, during these three weeks on Sinai, I have felt alone, absolutely, miserably alone. *(To the audience)* You don't know what it is. You can't know . . . no, don't seek any comparison in your daily existence. In the course of this existence one never feels truly alone . . . I'm serious. One finds himself sometimes, one believes himself sometimes far removed from everything and everybody . . . but if one questions the things around him, and especially, the solitude which seems to smother him, he feels quite sincerely that near or far there are things, there are animals, there are beings to receive the words he might utter and send them back to him . . . With Him, no such thing. Just imagine, just try to imagine what one of those absences means. You can't possibly understand it. Gone! Vanished! Disappeared! And where is He now? You can look for Him if you care to, but you'll not find Him. Say, at this very moment, if you lean your head back, as I'm doing, see . . . *(He leans back.)* you feel all of a sudden — and it sends chills down your spine — that above your head among the swirling clouds, there is nothing — nothing at all, except an immense hole, opened in the clouds, really wide open in the sky, through which the indifference of an . . . unsympathetic firmament pours down on you like an avalanche of snow. The Lord, for a brief time, has disappeared from the world. *(He gets up and walks, thinking.)* You know what I think? Do you know what I think when He goes off like that without any warning? Well, I think He has gone, for a short time, to direct another universe . . . or some other universes similar to our own or different from it. Why not different? Ours, you know, is not such a howling success. Afterwards, for some reason which I can't fathom, but which exists — yes, exists — He rushes back to us, and there is, once again, someone behind that hole in the sky. There! Do you follow me? It's as simple as that, and that explains every unexplainable and incomprehensible thing that happens in this world — and no doubt, in the others. *(He sits down again. Pause)* You see, if I had the time, if I weren't always bothered and pestered by the thousand things I have to do, I would try to formulate very clearly my theory on the presence and absence of God in the world. It would be my little cosmogony, why not? And it would startle a lot

of people, who think I'm nothing more than a clumsy old man, and not a very smart one either. The main idea would be the trip that God takes from time to time, from one universe to another universe, every time He feels the need. What need? You ask me. Aha! That, I don't know, but all at once, God feels this need to leave for . . . somewhere else, for one of those worlds which we don't know and will never know, but which exists nonetheless. And God changes His residence. That's it. There's no longer a God watching over us, in our heaven. *The Absences of God.* What a title, eh, on the cover of a book! *(He laughs. A short time passes.)* These absences of God, that explains why certain times you can pray all you want, until your throat gets dry, laying your soul bare, and get no results, there's a wall around you and your prayer comes back to you stamped "Return to sender." Other times, as soon as the first word leaves your lips, you have the answer — good or bad, that's another matter, but at least you have the answer: it means that your prayer surged forth into the air surrounding you and found the great, divine ear wide open. You've surely experienced that. *(As in a dream)* The absences of God! That's also what explains why there are in the world some times when peace abounds and others when war rages. The same is true for catastrophes . . . tidal waves, earthquakes, floods, and so on, which, according to the good folks, occur in series. That's the time when God is off tending another flock. Your own people can wear their throats out with prayers and supplications: there's nothing at the end of the hole, except the icy splendor of celestial solitude. Where is God? Well, where *is* He? I no longer feel His presence. Confound it! God is gone. God is traveling. *(A rather long time passes; he gets up, then comes slowly downstage facing the audience.)* The mistake, of course, was to initiate the dialogue at the wrong moment, I mean, at the moment when both He and I had grave concerns. And naturally, I don't count: as soon as He speaks, everything yields within me, everything falls apart, comes undone . . . so anxious am I to devote myself to His service. I erase everything, I cleanse myself of everything and then . . . "Present!" . . . But Him, I'm just not sure. At that moment, there are things which don't quite fall into place and which preoccupy Him. I get . . . the impression . . . yes, that's it: the impression that at the instant He called me, He was on the verge of leaving . . . on one of His . . . tours. Oh, I know Him, all right. He knows me, that's certain, but I know Him too. That way of expressing Himself, that hesitation, that reservation which I sense behind the words He utters, and that's it! I've got it. He's distracted. He's somewhere else. He's doing one thing while thinking of something else. He attacks everything indirectly, in a roundabout manner, if I may say so. In short, He's slipping away. Then, you tell me, and I say it too, then why summon me to this mountaintop, to receive the law? Why light that mysterious fire — extinguished, as you can see, for a long time now—that fire which gave me the illusion of His presence? During our conversations, you saw it yourself, He was never here . . . never completely here. He was here, though, His attention half turned out into space and completely preoccupied with the idea that He had something to do elsewhere! So? So?

I had to figure it out all alone, without anybody helping me in any way, I provided my own support, my own encouragement, my own comfort . . . twenty times a day. Three weeks for fifteen lines of writing! I know plenty of authors who are more prolific! Well, that's it, it's over. But is it? Is it completely over, without a postscript or an appendix? *Ne varietur?* Throughout eternity? That's what I'd like to know! *(He listens.)* Complete silence. Nobody's on the phone. *(He sighs.)* My, my! What else can I do now? *(He sits down, hides his face in his hands. A short time passes.)* Everything is on it . . . written on these two tablets . . . *(He holds them up.)* . . . everything He told me at least. And what more can you do? If He had, let's say . . . some things to add, others to clarify, still others to emphasize, I should have been told! But who, besides Him, knows what He wants? Oh, I really wish I knew what He wanted, because it's serious, you know. If I carry back an altered document to those down below and they find out, good heavens, can you imagine the scandal? A contrived scandal, but a scandal just the same. Some people, who could not really care a hill of beans about the word of God, would claim that I am turning that word to my own advantage; other loudmouths would demand, while banging on the table, that I be indicted immediately. In short, everyone would make a senseless clamor! Without realizing that the most furious one, even of all of them, would be Him. Him, with that bad temper which astonishes me and has always astonished me . . . Him, with his sense of justice . . . oh, it's certain . . . but a certain justice which has no relationship to what the others of us call by that lofty name . . . Him, especially, with that way of unleashing His frightful wrath all at once for some little thing that you forget to do, for some little word you fail to say. And right away, a tongue lashing, "All right, Moses, what's up? What's happening? You couldn't possibly suspect that I hadn't finished, that I needed a little time to think, a little time to meditate, to dally over everything I have left to say. Ah, Moses, in spite of your being an old fellow, you're as light-headed as a youngster!" . . . and other compliments of the same nature. That's the way He is. *(Tenderly)* Ah, yes, that's the way He is . . . and these compliments, He has paid them to me twenty times . . . and then right after that *(He sighs)* comes one of those great punishments of which He holds the secret: without mincing words, He smites the first-born of each family, at the same time He slays, very quietly, the first-born of every kind of animal . . . or else it's the sudden appearance, then the propagation of a tremendous thing like, for example, the great leprosy, or . . . well, you see what I mean. Admit it, just between us, it's not easy to serve Him, even when you love Him, as I do, to the point of consecrat-ing your life to Him. *(Suddenly, changing his tone)* He definitely is not here. I admit I rather forced the issue of recriminations, a matter of putting His power to the test. If He had heard me, just think! A long time ago, sleepy or alert, He would have sent me, by the quickest route, a . . . sign, a memory aid, preferably painful, to call me back to order. My old neuralgia would have split my head from ear to ear or else my sciatica would have sent pains through my thigh like a red hot iron. Not to mention a little warning roll of thunder or bolt of lightning. No, you see, He's not here, He's gone. And I have nothing else to do except go back down below and find my folks. My God, how that bothers me, if you only knew. It drains me! Weighs heavy on me! And beats me down! Oh, why couldn't I just remain the man I once was! But you have to realize that it's for Him . . . to serve Him that I've become the man I am today, this sort of assistant, or school principal, or rather bur-sar, that's it, a greedy bursar who keeps a sharp eye on the expenditures, holds the receipts in a clawlike grip, scolds this per-son, reprimands that one, in a nutshell, puts order in the finances and administra-tion of the household. A kind of general bursar and superintendent. That's not the way to gain friends, I must confess. When I think that I was brought up to live away from the limelight, far from the crowd, appreciat-ing and cherishing the life we've been given to live, simply! Oh, well, that's the way it is . . .

Now I have to go down, I have to report to the people down there the . . . fruits of my journey. It's a pity. I would gladly stay here waiting for God to come back to me. Poor God! He certainly thinks — and I understand it—that He has brought a lot of honor to the people of Israel by dictating His law to me, and that these people, wide-eyed with admiration, wild with gratitude, will throw themselves flat on their bellies, with their noses in the dust at the first words I shall utter . . . and all will shout "Glory to God!" He is convinced that I'll hurry to go down into the valley and assemble the tribes.

I'm going down, all right, but without haste or a true desire, going down, yes, and I repeat, it's a pity. I have enjoyed life on Sinai, during my three-week retreat. I've worshiped God as never before, and I've been happy, if I may say so, excluding, of course, the sudden pangs of anguish which came to me each time His voice grew distant, to the point of disappearing. In addition, this stay on the mountain has been for me, I dare say it, healthy, and it allowed me to notice how very few things are necessary in order to keep oneself alive —look at me! *(He sticks out his chest.)* A creature of God. I'll give you the recipe: a few roots as tender and tasty as asparagus, too (there are more than people think), plus two or three bunches a day of that good mountain grass, freshly picked and washed in three or four drops of spring water, you'll see, it's edible and even palatable. And that's more than enough.

Of course, it's not equivalent to lobster Newburg or breaded prawn, but I'll tell you one thing: beware of gastronomy. It's through it that the other sensual desires creep inside you, and you know He doesn't like sensual desires. No, not at all. There, enough talking. Now, I'm going down. They must be wondering down there what could have become of me! *(He takes a few steps toward the left wings, stops abruptly. With great emotion)* My God, my Lord God Almighty, wherever You are, hear me: in whatever place in this world or another world, even if You're in the vicinity of the planet Mars or . . . the nebula of Andromeda, if indeed there exists a region in Your sacred heaven which bears that lovely name, grant that a little bit, at least, of this prayer that I raise to You may reach You. I'm not asking much, nothing but a little word. Tell me only one little word, so that I may definitely know that my mission on this mountain is completed . . . the way You wanted it to be. Tell me the word! Tell it to me quickly, as You wish, however it will be easier or more agreeable for You to say it: drop it, toss it, throw it, spit it, vomit it, let it just fall, but let me have it, let me hear it. *(Forcefully)* Let me hear it! *(He stands listening, motionless, his hands on his hips and his head thrown back. A short time passes. He listens intensely. Angrily)* Nothing! Absolutely nothing! No need to insist, He's not there, He's no longer there. He's gone about His business, leaving me here all alone. *(He heaves a great sigh, calms down.)* Here comes one of those moments when there's no longer a God in heaven. I warn you: anything can happen! *(He walks toward the left wings and exits repeating)* Anything can happen!

curtain

ACT V

The assembly room, just as it was in the third act, well furnished, merry, noisy. In the middle of the room, a few carpenters are busy building a kind of substructure, which will serve as a pedestal for the statue of the golden calf, which will be brought in later. They are helped by several more or less efficient people who, apparently, are possessed by that spirit of enterprise and solidarity which suddenly inspires men as soon as they set out to play a trick on someone. This golden calf is their victory, all the more precious since Aaron was hoodwinked. As the curtain rises, the din of hammerblows and diverse cries is heard. A short time passes.

SIMEON: *(Entering from upstage, triumphantly)* And here's the hammer!

SEVERAL VOICES: Ah! the hammer! Hurrah! Hurrah! Here's the hammer!

SIMEON: *(To Gaddi, near the pedestal)* Your wife didn't want to let me have it. Ha! ha!

VOICES: Ha! ha!

SIMEON: *(Laughing)* She told me she didn't know what I intended to do with that hammer . . . and that when you left, you took away all the hammers from the house *(General laughter)*

GADDI: *(Coldly)* All right. So what?

SIMEON: So I pushed her aside.

GADDI: *(Furious)* What do you mean, "pushed her aside"?

SIMEON: Calm down. I didn't touch her.

I pushed her without touching her the least in the world, without even brushing against her, merely by taking a step toward her. She backed away.

GADDI: *(Still very coldly)* I know she can't stand for people to touch her. *(Very dryly)* Well, are you going to pass me that hammer?

SIMEON: *(Hastily)* Here, take it. *(He hands it to him.)* I went straight to it, right where you said it would be — above and to the right of the work bench, between a small saw and an assortment of screwdrivers. Old boy, that's some collection you've got!

GADDI: What?

SIMEON: Screwdrivers. *(To the others)* You've never seen the like!

(Gaddi taps the hammer against the pedestal. A short time passes.)

SIMEON: Say, Gaddi.

GADDI: Yeah.

SIMEON: Your wife's really devoted to Moses, eh?

GADDI: Did she tell you that?

SIMEON: No, what do *you* think, not exactly. But then, about the calf, she said a mouthful! It's a mistake, an error, a crime and what's more, an unwarranted expense. I can hear her now.

GADDI: So can I!

SIMEON: *(Imitating Gaddi's wife)* "An unwarranted expense!" And as for us, we're just a band of ignorant imbeciles. I tell you, Gaddi, I didn't know where to hide.

GADDI: *(Sighing)* Yes, oh, I know her like

a book. I've been knowing for twenty years that I didn't marry a compatible woman. *(He resumes his tapping with the hammer. Someone begins singing. A short time passes. Nadab enters from upstage rear amid a joyous tumult of laughter, songs, and hammerblows.)*

NADAB: *(Very lively)* All right! I see we're working joyfully. *(He comes to the pedestal. Rather briskly)* Well, is everything okay?

GADDI: *(Unemotionally)* It's okay.

NADAB: What's the matter? You look upset!

GADDI: I'm uneasy. I think we're wrong.

NADAB: What do you mean "wrong"?

GADDI: Hm? Well, yes . . . I wonder . . .

NADAB: You wonder?

GADDI: Whether we're right to do what we're doing. Suppose he comes back.

NADAB: Who?

GADDI: Why, Moses. Who else? What if he were to come back all of a sudden? Have you ever seen him when he's angry?

NADAB: Him? Why, at least twenty times! And I mean really angry, you can take it from me. His eyes flashed fire, and he roared loud enough to make the house fall down.

GADDI: Did it fall down?

NADAB: No, of course not. It's a way of speaking.

GADDI: Well, this time it will fall down. If he ever comes back and sees how we have behaved, we're really in for a storm.

NADAB: *(Laughing)* Come now!

GADDI: Come now? You'll see, Nadab, a violent storm . . .

NADAB: *(Forcefully)* Don't get yourself all worked up. Where Moses is at this moment, there Moses will remain. He will remain there in silence until the . . . resurrection. What's more . . . *(He stops.)*

GADDI: What's more?

NADAB: There's nothing to fear from Moses, his brother is with us.

GADDI: He is not with us. We duped . . . how shall I put it? *You* made him swallow, with a cunning that frightened me, a sugar-coated pill. If he only knew. . . .

NADAB: If he only knew what?

GADDI: The real importance of the golden calf, in our eyes . . . and that, without seeming to do so, we're secretly getting ready to make it the new god of our nation.

NADAB: *(Interrupting him)* You don't know how the man's mind works. Just think! Rather than look like an idiot in the eyes of his brother, Aaron would prefer, I don't know . . . to join the opposition and side with us.

GADDI: I certainly hope so, but before the golden calf is placed on the altar, I'm sending a prayer up to the ex-Lord: "My God, grant that this may not happen."

NADAB: *(Smiling)* I confess, I don't believe much more in the golden calf than I did in the Lord, but I can reassure you: that will not happen.

GADDI: Hmph!

NADAB: I guarantee it. *(He starts to walk away but returns.)* Your wife is responsible for this uneasiness?

GADDI: *(Quickly)* No, no . . .

NADAB: Women, you know, they're

coming into their own! *(He walks away and goes to join the other workers near the pedestal. To Dan)* So, the work is progressing?

DAN: It's coming along all right.

NADAB: It has to, and quickly, because in less than thirty minutes, the golden calf will be here.

DAN: *(Surprised)* Already?

NADAB: Yes, already, it's finished. I've just been to take a look at it in the hangar of the firehouse. They were getting it ready.

CALEB: Is it pretty?

NADAB: I think it's superb.

CALEB: Tell me, Nadab, if it's not being indiscreet, who made it?

NADAB: The golden calf? What, you don't know?

CALEB: No.

VOICES: We don't either . . . that's right! Who made the golden calf?

NADAB: *(Laughing)* Can it be that you really don't know? Why, Aaron made it.

CALEB: No!

VOICES: Really? Aaron, Moses' brother?

NADAB: Moses' brother, Aaron.

CALEB: Did you see him do it?

NADAB: I realize it's hard to believe, but there's not a shadow of a doubt on this subject. What's more, it's in the Bible.

CALEB: The Bible?

NADAB: Yes, don't you know what that is?

VOICES: The Bible! Seems it's in the Bible . . .

SODI: I have one on me. Every morning and evening I read a short passage from

it. It's educational. And you can find in it a solution for everything that happens to you.

NADAB: Is that so! Well, hand it to me. *(Passing from hand to hand, the Bible reaches him. He opens it, leafs through it.)* Let's see. Here. It's the thirty-second verse of the book of Exodus . . . listen . . . I'll read it: "And all (all, that's you) and all took off the golden rings which were on their ears; and they brought them to Aaron." *(He repeats, emphasizing.)* To Aaron.

CALEB: Well, that doesn't mean . . .

NADAB: *(Interrupting him)* Wait a second! Impatient friend. *(He reads.)* " . . . to Aaron, who took them from their hands, fashioned them with the chisel and made of them a cast of a calf . . ." It couldn't be clearer.

CALEB: *(Hardly convinced)* Probably, probably. Maybe it's clear, but it's still unusual.

NADAB: The Bible is full of unusual things.

CALEB: Even so, Nadab, even so! Aaron, Moses' brother, more than his brother — his confidant, his buddy, his right-hand man. It's unbelievable that he allowed us, without balking too much, to detach ourselves from Moses. But to drop him straight out, to the point of betraying him, that's even more difficult to understand. And when it comes to his making the symbol of betrayal with his own hands, I confess that I don't understand anymore.

NADAB: What's that? What betrayal? I told him distinctly that the golden calf would only be the sign, the symbol of our work, our daily preoccupations. He believed me, the good fellow.

CALEB: But when he realizes . . .

NADAB: Why should he realize it? Aaron is a naïve man. You'd think his brother created him for his own personal usage. Calm down! Everything will turn out fine, you'll see. *(He walks away. Resumption of the hammerblows. A short time passes. Nadab, walking among the others, shakes a few hands. Suddenly, a distant trumpet fanfare pierces the atmosphere. Nadab gives a start and yells.)* What is that? *(An abrupt silence, during which the trumpets are heard more clearly. Their sound suggests a parade.)* Hm? Say, what is it?

MANASSEH: Sounds like trumpets.

NADAB: *(Sarcastically)* I never would have guessed that. *(Serious)* What do they mean, those trumpets? *(He goes quickly upstage toward the door at the rear, and just as he is about to leave, he is jostled by a messenger who comes running in.)*

MESSENGER: *(Out of breath)* Here it comes! Here it comes!

NADAB: What?

MESSENGER: The golden calf.

NADAB: Those fanfares are for it?

MESSENGER: Why, what else? The whole village is giving a parade to honor it.

NADAB: What nonsense! I was very careful to specify — no hoopla or ceremony. Simply! In all modesty! Ah, I wish I knew . . . *(The fanfare comes closer. Two men run in.)*

FIRST MAN: Here it is!

SECOND MAN: It's here!

NADAB: *(Exasperated)* All right. Now calm down! . . . Yes, I'd really like to know who could have taken it upon himself to let loose all this commotion . . . *(The fanfare gets even louder while the din rises in the assembly room. Noise of voices, shouts and laughter. Nadab, unable to stand it any longer, stands firmly on the threshold, facing the outside; then, in a thundering voice, addresses those in the parade.)* Enough! *(The trumpets stop irregularly, one after the other.)* Enough, I said! *(Relative silence. Still on the threshold, he speaks to the crowd outside.)* Everybody, go back home! *(Murmurs from the crowd)* I said everybody! Women, children, old men, all of you, go home. You may return later, when you are told.

A VOICE: *(Outside)* You won't tell us anything!

ANOTHER VOICE: You never tell us anything!

NADAB: You may return when we have installed the statue in this hall. Not before! *(The crowd murmurs. Nadab raises his voice.)* Why, what is the meaning of this display of independence, of anarchy that you have revealed in the last month? I am here to inform you that it won't work. Now go home! You can see that the hall is too small to hold all of you! Come now, go back home! Only the bearers of the statue will get in here. Is that understood? No exceptions! *(He comes inside again and speaks to those assembled.)* What idiot got the bright idea to call all those people together! That racket! Listen to that! Well, are they leaving or not? We've got enough problems to solve without people inventing some for us. *(He goes back to the door and looks outside.)* They're dispersing, good, but with a prudent slowness. And they don't seem happy. *(He yells.)* Come! Let's get a move on. An hour from now, you can come back. Good! Now the bearers will enter slowly, give them time to turn around. There, that's it! *(Four men enter, carrying on their shoulders a kind of stretcher bearing the golden calf. The statue is very stylized, and, apparently, owes nothing to Michelangelo or even Bourdelle.)* I said slowly! You're moving too fast. *(Setting the pace)* There! There! And you'll lay your burden down here. *(On the pedestal)* Fine! Now all you have to do is remove the stretcher . . . Easy! . . . Easy! That's it. Well, gentlemen, that's a fine looking calf! *(Applause from the others)* Come on in, Aaron! Come behold your work. *(Aaron enters from upstage center.)* Well, Aaron, I didn't know you were so talented.

AARON: It's not very much.

NADAB: Not very much, you say! Would you have preferred making us a whole herd? *(He laughs.)*

AARON: You're still joking. Listen, I'm uneasy.

NADAB: What a strange thing to say!

AARON: Maybe I shouldn't have . . .

NADAB: What?

AARON: I . . . can't quite put it into words. I have the impression, well . . . of having done something I shouldn't have done.

NADAB: Nonsense! Quite simply, you

fashioned with your hands the thing . . . needed to keep peace among a band of squawkers who are hard to manage.

AARON: *(Sighing)* Let's suppose that's true. Now what?

NADAB: Now? We're going to give them . . .

AARON: The squawkers?

NADAB: The squawkers . . . give them permission to celebrate the arrival of the golden calf among us — music, dancing, songs, in fact, all the usual ways men have of expressing their joy — or simply their pleasure.

AARON: I have a better idea. I believe we should, first of all, offer a sacrifice to the Lord. *(A short time passes.)* I'm going to build an altar. . . .

NADAB: Oh, no, Aaron, you've done enough building! No more building! You are tireless! Allow us, if you will, to keep a little distance from the presence of God. *(To the others)* Come, my friends, let everyone prepare to honor the calf! To dance for the calf! All together, we're going to celebrate the golden calf.

AARON: Why no, no!

NADAB: *(Yelling)* Come, come, take your place! The ritual dance of the grass and the green prairie! In honor of the golden calf and his creator, Aaron, the Levite!

AARON: Not on your life! Let me out of here . . .

NADAB: I'd like to see that. Ready! Begin! 1, 2, 3, 4, . . . 1, 2, 3, 4, . . . *(He begins to dance; two beats per leg: 1, 2, for the left leg; 3, 4, for the right. He seizes one of Aaron's arms and, at the same moment,*

Manasseh takes Aaron's other arm. Aaron, who resists at first, quickly stops resisting and dances like the others. In a few seconds, the dance is general: 1, 2, 3, 4 . . . 1, 2, 3, 4. People from the outside appear at the door, look into the hall, come in yelling and join in the dancing: 1, 2, 3, 4 . . . 1, 2, 3, 4. A reasonable time of general dancing passes. Suddenly, Moses appears in the upstage center doorway. No one sees him. He has in his arms the tablets of the Law. He observes the dancing for an instant as it gets more and more frenzied, then he makes his way to the dais and mounts it. A short time passes.)

MOSES: *(Yelling)* Aaron! *(Louder)* Aaron, brother of Moses!

AARON: I am here . . . *(He looks in the direction of the voice, sees Moses and groans.)* Oh, my God! *(He extricates himself from the arms of Manasseh and Nadab, shouting.)* Stop! Stop! Look who's here. Look who's come back! My God, what have you done? What have you made me do?

(The dancers, having stopped abruptly, look at Moses and lower their heads. Aaron rushes past the groups, comes to the edge of the dais and kneels. Total silence)

MOSES: *(His voice breaking with emotion, he stops often, as if to compose himself.)* If you are not yet . . . reduced to ashes, yes . . . consumed even to your bones . . . burnt up in flames and smoke by the fire of divine wrath and vengeance . . . it's because I knew, before entering this hall, what I would find here — a band, a coterie, a pack of renegades! What else can you call those who renege on their word and their religion? *(Very familiar, suddenly)* And I warn you, don't act smart with me, for it's not too late, it's never too late to punish the guilty, especially those who, like you, can offer no kind of excuse. *(He emphasizes.)* No kind of excuse.

AARON: Moses!

MOSES: You, leave! Get up and leave.

AARON: But . . .

MOSES: Get out of my sight!

(Aaron gets up and steps aside. Moses addresses the others.) By the silence and calm that reign here, or that seem to reign here, you might suppose that I have already interceded for you and that God has heard me. And that's exactly what has happened. God, for a short time, is giving you credit, but only for a short time, until I have drawn out into the open the things that took place in my absence. Meanwhile, God has withdrawn. He has withdrawn as the sea recedes, leaving between Him and you a sort of vast, damp beach, where the slightest misstep would leave an imprint. But God is there, on the horizon, foaming and roaring as the sea foams and roars while waiting to charge forth in the attack on the pale shores. To think, to think that for decades I have done the impossible in order to instill within you my notion of an all-powerful God and not one of you has followed me, not even Aaron, not even my own brother, whom I thought so close to me!

NADAB: Don't say such things. He was hoodwinked.

MOSES: Who's that speaking?

NADAB: Aaron didn't know what it was all about. *(He takes a few steps toward the dais.)*

MOSES: Why, it's Mr. Nadab! The ineffable Mr. Nadab, who always shows up in the nick of time.

NADAB: It's only to tell you . . .

MOSES: Silence!

NADAB: . . . that Aaron is not guilty. It's a trick that was played on him.

MOSES *(Quite distinctly)* Really? When my eyes gazed through that door just now, what was Aaron doing?

NADAB: How should I know?

MOSES: Well, *I* know, *I* saw him. It's odd, he was the first one I saw. He was kicking up his heels with the others; he was kicking up his heels just like the others. That's what he was doing.

NADAB: That doesn't mean anything.

MOSES: Oh, no? Then what does mean something?

NADAB: There aren't just facts, there are intentions.

MOSES: *(Sarcastic)* His were pure? *(To Aaron, abruptly)* Speak up, Aaron!

AARON: What's the use? You won't listen to me.

MOSES: I always listen. Then I speak.

AARON: Or just the opposite?

MOSES: What do you mean "the opposite"?

AARON: I mean you speak first and then you try to understand, but only when it suits you.

MOSES: My question is quite simple: I'm asking to be told right away how in three weeks a little more than three weeks, the whole . . . monument, the lofty construction, the moral architecture that I had bequeathed to the Jewish nation when I left has suddenly collapsed, ruined from top to bottom, to the extent that now you're wallowing in the dust and debris.

It couldn't be more simple. *(He breathes as if exasperated, then, changes his tone.)* Why, you blooming idiots, it was God *(Emphasizing)*, God. Do you realize? God Himself who informed me of your betrayal, of your cowardice. So what need have I to try to understand? Understand what? In the first place, He wasn't there. There was no one there anymore. *(He takes a deep breath. Then, more calmly)* After I don't know how many attempts on my part to reach the divine ear, suddenly, abruptly . . . and I assure you it was a marvelous moment for me . . . I understood, I sensed that at last the line was open. A marvelous moment, I repeat: a door, a skylight suddenly opened right above my head, through which the voice of God showered down on me like summer rain . . . a gentle summer rain. And He told me: "Go down, Moses (I was away on Sinai), go down, because your people whom you led out of the land of Egypt, your people have become corrupted . . ." How? I yelled. "They have made for themselves a golden calf and have prostrated themselves before it . . ."

NADAB: No, not prostrated — we just danced.

MOSES: Who dares to keep talking?

NADAB: Just danced, like we did at the feast of spring, the dance of the green prairie.

MOSES: Why, of course, it's still good Mr. Nadab who feels the need to speak for all.

NADAB: Yes, it's me and I say there was nothing in what we did worthy of whipping a cat.

MOSES: Look inside yourself, liar! Not worthy of whipping a cat? Dare repeat it.

NADAB: It was a very innocent game . . . as are most of our popular dances.

MOSES: Look deep inside yourself!

NADAB: All right, I'm looking.

MOSES: What do you see? Dare tell me that when I arrived just now you were *just* dancing, with vim and vigor, like we dance in the spring.

NADAB: *(Hesitating)* Maybe not quite, but . . .

MOSES: *(Shouting)* Not at all, you mean! That dance was preparing . . . that dance, it was obvious, was leading up to a totally blissful submission . . . kneeling . . . surrender.

NADAB: And when would that take place?

MOSES: *(Giving vent to his anger)* Listen, make him shut up! Let those here present who love this man keep him from talking or else I'll . . . I'll bash his face in!

NADAB: You'd still have to be able to . . . *(The three or four men near Nadab rush on him and silence him.)*

MOSES: Good. *(A short time passes.)* Now to finish, the Lord told me: "I have looked upon this nation, and behold it is a stiff-necked nation."

(Reaction among those present. Everybody is questioning his neighbor. Efforts are made to prove the suppleness of their necks. Great murmuring) You have a stiff neck. It can't be helped; God told me so Himself. And He added, "Now leave them to Me. Let My wrath blaze forth and let Me consume them." Ah! poor Israelites! If ever you came close to being roasted alive it was at that moment. God thundered fire and smoke. He was nothing but flames. Fire shot from His eyes and from His mouth. Each word He uttered was accompanied by a flame, as long as that *(He indicates a length of about a foot and a half.)* which spewed from His mouth and sputtered in the air. At that moment, without weighing the situation or thinking, I fell on my knees. The idea had struck me that death by fire is a terrible death, a frightful death. "Lord!" I screamed. "Give heed to my question. Why would You turn Your wrath against Your people, whom You have brought out of the land of Egypt? Remember Abraham, Isaac and Jacob, Your servants, with whom You made a covenant, telling them, 'I will multiply your seed like the stars in the heavens . . . ' Now, listen to that!" . . . Then God repented. Repented, completely. What do you say about that? God repented of the evil that He had said He would do to His people. Now you can see what's good, what's excellent about God. He doesn't need speeches. All you have to do is touch the right cord. If you touch the right cord, one word, a single one, is enough. Now, I touched the right cord by reminding the Lord of His promise concerning your seed. And God repented! *(He takes a few steps to the right and to the left,*

as if a prey to his thoughts.) You see, I'm an old man. Since I've been keeping company with God, I've seen—I can say this—a little of everything. But never before had I seen such an unbelievable thing — the repentance of God. Are you aware of everything that means in simplicity, in modesty, in humility on His part? He went too far . . . in the . . . calculation of His possibilities and then He stopped. He thought. He backed away, beating His chest, like a common sinner, like you, like me, like anyone in the world might do, no matter how little honesty or good faith he possessed. God, however, who is Total Perfection, did not hesitate one second to erase a thought which He judged rash, unjust or simply ill-conceived. He erased it with one stroke, meditated for a moment, then He found another, which, this time, suited Him and was also in keeping with the idea that He holds of divine justice. What a lesson, my friends! What a magnificent lesson of . . . of divineness! *(He cries out.)* Oh God! *(He falls to his knees; everybody imitates him, except Nadab who remains standing in a corner.)* Grant that we may thank You for being what You are, grant that we may worship You, as You deserve to be worshiped, without restriction or self-interest, but with our entire souls, Lord! *(A short time of silent meditation, then Moses gets up briskly, addresses those gathered.)* Don't move! Don't move at all! You are as you should be, in the position necessary to receive that which I went to seek atop Mt. Sinai, and which I am going to give you. *(With appropriate solemnity)* It concerns the Law of God, His Ten Commandments, written on these two slabs of stone, which are henceforth the Tablets of the Law. All of you, remain on your knees! *(A man in the crowd gets up with apparent difficulty.)* What's the matter with you over there? Didn't you hear what I said?

MAN: My knees hurt.

MOSES: Nonsense!

MAN: I swear it. This morning the doctor that came to see me told me I had a case of rheumatism. Rheumatism *(Stammering)* in my joints and I'm s'pose' to sit down or maybe lay down when it's both'in' me.

MOSES: Whereupon, of course, you hastened to get up and come here to admire the calf. Maybe you even danced?

MAN: No, just a few steps.

MOSES: Well, then take just a few more steps, which will carry you out of this hall. *(He talks with more authority.)* Go on, move! Out! Out! *(He takes a step toward the man.)* Are you going to clear out? You're not worthy to be here. *(The man rushes out.)* If there is anyone else afflicted like that braggart with such rheumatism *(Imitating the man)* "in his joints" that he cannot remain kneeling, let him get up and leave the hall . . . No one? *(To Nadab, who is standing with his chest out, almost defiantly)* Oh, yes, Nadab, my good friend, I notice that you are standing, but you and I have a private score that we'll settle later. Besides, you are the unbeliever, the typical unbeliever, that is to say, the alien element needed in a meeting of believers to make the members interact with one another and, if I may say so, to unite them into a more solid coalition. So, no one else wants to get up? Or leave? Perfect. Here, then, is the Decalogue. It's about, as I told you, the commandments of God. There are ten. God dictated them to me in a very unusual manner: one, then another, then another, still another . . . and, between two commandments, there might be an interval of a day, sometimes even of several, which explains why I stayed up there so long. Another observation: the order of the commandments is not that in which they were dictated. I am the one who after thinking about it . . . *(He interrupts himself. Changing his tone)* Ah, listen, that's enough! If there are those among you who have St. Vitus's dance, let them arise and leave this hall. You can't imagine how annoying it is for me to see heads constantly moving. It's like being on the edge of a field when the storm hits and the wind rises. *(Dryly)* Come, enough!

(Everybody remains motionless in total silence.) Attention, now. *(Reading from one of the tablets)* "I am the Lord, thy God, who brought thee out of the land of Egypt, out of the house of bondage . . ." *(He stops reading.)* Now, that's the introduction. In reality, God didn't put it in His commandments, I'm the one who added that, because that's the way He addressed me, when He had something to tell me.

NADAB: On those occasions when you were perhaps mistaken and probably took Him for somebody else.

MOSES: Shut up, you idiot! *(To the others)* Here is the first commandment: *(Reading)* "Thou shalt have no other gods before me." *(He stops reading.)* That's self-explanatory. Then comes the development of this first commandment; it is interpreted this way *(Reading):* "Thou shalt not make unto thee any graven image or any likeness of anything that is in heaven above, or that is in the earth beneath, or that is in the water, under the earth."

NADAB: *(Correcting Moses)* "Under the sea," you mean.

MOSES: No, under the *earth*. After all, I *can* read.

NADAB: Granted. Now, if I understand clearly this divine language, God advocates the rapid and total destruction of the golden calf, a graven image in the likeness, etc., etc.

AARON: *(Unhappy)* That doesn't resemble a calf!

NADAB: But you wanted it to resemble one! Only the intention counts, ask your brother. So, we destroy the golden calf, and that's when we have our fun.

MOSES: Maybe not so much, you'll see. Second commandment. *(Reading)* "Thou shalt not take the name of the Lord thy God in vain, for the Lord will not hold him guiltless who takes His name in vain . . . "

NADAB: Oddly composed, that commandment. For after all, if the Lord forbids anybody to take His name in vain, it is quite evident that the one who does so cannot be held as innocent. But we can't force God to attend law school.

MOSES: *(Raising his voice)* Third commandment. *(Reading)* "Six days shalt thou labor and do all thy work; the seventh day is a sabbath to the Lord, thy God; on it thou shalt do no work, thou, nor thy son, nor thy daughter, nor thy manservant, nor thy maidservant, nor thy cattle, nor the sojourner who is within thy gates . . . "

NADAB: How about my wife? *(Laughter from some of those assembled)* I'm serious. How about my wife? The fact is, she's not mentioned in that passage. Is that an oversight, or was it done on purpose?

MOSES: *(Exasperated)* O my God, You have already granted me so much, grant me the patience to endure this babboon here until I finish! Fourth commandment. *(Reading)* "Honor thy father and thy mother, that thy days may be long upon the land . . . "

NADAB I beg you to forgive me, but I don't see the relationship. I see no relationship between the fact of being a good son and the fact of becoming a centenarian. *(General laughter)* Or else, God has some lucidity about filiation and longevity which I lack. *(To Moses)* Are you sure you wrote that down right?

MOSES: *(In a thundering voice)* Fifth commandment. It's brief, but it states clearly what it means. Listen. *(He takes a breath. Slowly and forcefully)* "Thou shalt not kill." *(A short time passes.)*

NADAB: *(Enthusiastically)* Bravo! That's the best one! *(Agitation in the group)* What! Men are killing each other, men are cutting each other's throats, men are ripping each other apart from one end of the planet to the other, and here he comes telling us that we mustn't do that because it's not right? And that God doesn't like to see that? *(The agitation increases; some people get up and converse. Nadab advances to the middle of the hall.)* Am I in a course of ethics in an elementary school or am I immersed, from head to toe, in the hard school of life, a ruthless life, which I must make for myself each day by myself while all my neighbors are determined to deprive me of it in order to take my place? I move that we delete this fifth commandment and replace it with another, which would begin like this: "War being the supreme law of the world . . . " (General applause. Everybody stands up.)*

MOSES: *(In the uproar)* Enough! Enough! You are not worthy . . . *(The uproar continues.)* I demand that there be silence . . . I command you to be quiet. . . . Will you be silent? *(The uproar continues. Moses screams.)* Nothing can be done with you! All that I have tried . . . all that I have undertaken, zero straight across the board. Always caught between the tree, which is God, and the bark, which is you! Always getting myself pinched. *(Crescendo)* I'm fed up! I'm fed up! I'm fed up! *(He takes the tablets of the Law and hurls them to the floor, where they break. A general silence follows this gesture. In the silence)* You may ask Nadab to give you some commandments which will be less inclined to excite your scoffing. *(A long time passes. Nadab, very sheepishly, joins Moses.)*

NADAB: *(With embarrassment)* I'm sorry, Moses.

MOSES: You're sorry! I would never have thought that it might touch you so deeply. *(Moses shrugs his shoulders, then goes* slowly near the golden calf. He looks at it. Still total silence) This whole mess for that! (He points to the calf.) Frankly, Aaron, you'll get no compliments from me. That represents everything they want, except the worthy son of a bull.

AARON: I keep telling them that. (He joins Moses. A short time passes.)

MOSES: The fact remains that if you had demonstrated more talent, we would have here, at this moment, a true calf, made of gold, and the object of general admiration and adoration.

AARON: They didn't insist on the calf! They didn't insist on it any more than I! A cow or a horse would have done just as well. If, in the end, they opted for the calf, it's because, being smaller, it required less gold. You know them. Maybe they are adventurous, I mean, capricious, daredevils, but above all, they're economical.

MOSES: Probably, probably, but all the same, it was you who gave form to their gold.

AARON: Please try to understand. They asked me to make them the image of a . . . companion, a sort of . . . witness to their daily existence. Never would I have believed that such a natural request . . . I was used like a simpleton.

(A short time. passes.)

MOSES: Yes, I'm beginning to see. I'm beginning to see how things happened. (Changing his tone, bruskly) Tell me, Aaron, do you want to help me?

AARON: Of course! Just name it.

MOSES: Let's knock down your masterpiece.

AARON: Gladly. That's all it deserves.

(Both of them put their backs against the calf, which, suddenly, gives way and topples down. A long murmur from the others)

MOSES: There! Now we can see better. (He turns toward the others.) Well, gentlemen, we have to face the issues. I came back just in time to keep you from committing an error, what am I saying, an error, a crime, an unpardonable crime — the cult of the Beast. And still I wonder whether, intending to commit it, you have not already committed that crime. So . . . follow me carefully. Now, here you all are, behind Nadab, in the situation of those pagan nations, the Philistines, for example, or the Amalekites, against whom we have been fighting for years merely because they worship idol gods. Well then, what about you? Confess that, for an idol god, the calf is getting along fine! (A rather long time passes. Everybody bows his head. He continues in a calm voice.) As far as I'm concerned, you are lost. If you do not believe in the reality of a God who has given you so much tangible proof of His existence, it's because you are lost. (A short time passes.) You must be sick. That's getting to the bottom of the matter. You're sick. That's all.

AARON: That's what I told them.

MOSES: You're terribly sick.

AARON: I told them that too.

MOSES: You are afflicted with human weakness. It's a hopeless illness, which, if it spreads, attacks the body of the State and leads quickly to decadence, then death. It is this illness which cuts, then beats down, one on top of the other, all the civilizations of the world. All, or nearly all, are good in principle, but human weakness is there, with its parade of lesser vices: envy, jealousy, anger, ambition; invisible, yet present; like the worm inside the fruit, it ruins everything. Now . . . *(A short time passes.)* Now, what shall we do with you? Shall I harden my heart? Shall I persist in helping you out . . . in pulling you out of the hole? In the past, I would have done it. A long time ago, when we lived together the fine years of our heroic age. Today, now that I've grown old and weariness stiffens my bones, I'm going to sit down by the side of the road that you take and watch you go off to face your destiny. Spitefully, watch you go forth to face the future.

NADAB: Say! Wait a minute, I beg of you.

MOSES: Well, well. There he is again. What do you want now?

NADAB: A correction. The Bible doesn't say that.

MOSES: ''That'' what?

NADAB: That you watch us leave.

MOSES: Don't worry about it. I'm the one who writes the Bible.

NADAB: That's very convenient.

MOSES: Shut up! Let me see! Let me look . . . let me cast my glance into the destiny of this nation . . . I see! . . . Listen to me! It is what God orders, it is what the God you offended requires. Let me first tell you a sure thing. Listen. Never shall you enter the Promised Land. *(Murmur from the crowd)* Perhaps, after centuries, you will come close to it. Maybe even one day, you will sneak into it. But you will always feel yourselves on the verge of leaving it again,

as if you were caught red-handed in territorial theft, as if you occupied a strange land illegally. Because one thing is certain *(Forcefully)*: you will never — never — own the Promised Land.

NADAB: *(In a sharp voice)* So what? We'll go somewhere else. What difference does that make to us?

VOICES IN THE CROWD: Silence! Silence!

NADAB: I wouldn't even be sorry to have — for my own part . . .

VOICES: *(More numerous)* Enough! Enough! Silence!

MOSES: That is your punishment. In that way God is chastising you for having doubted Him: you'll never reach the Promised Land. You'll wander, I can see that, you'll wander all your life, not only your life, but that of your children, your children's children and so on until the end of time. I see you wandering, I am following you, I'm walking behind you in the course of the centuries. You are a wandering people. *(A trumpet fanfare begins very far away — scarcely audible — in the tempo of a slow march.)*

NADAB: Bah! We'll surely end up arriving somewhere!

MOSES: You'll never arrive. You're on the threshold of an immense journey, which will never end, and will carry you to every continent in the world. Europe, Africa, Asia . . . there'll be Jews all over the world.

NADAB: As for me, I like traveling. *(Nervously)* I like traveling a lot. *(Murmur from the crowd)* You like it too. We'll pitch our tents under all the skies around the globe and, wherever we go . . .

MOSES: *(Interrupting him)* You will not travel as others do. You'll be migrants. Endlessly and relentlessly, you'll migrate. Even when you think you're settled on some patch of land, you'll feel something move inside you — an uneasiness in your heart, a restlessness in your legs which will make you stand up if you're seated and will put you on the move again if you're standing. Like the wandering Jew, you'll have the traveler's staff in your hand, and on your back, in a sack, you'll carry your belongings. *(Trumpets closer)* Such is the punishment that is inflicted on you, the chastisement that God metes out to the worshipers of the golden calf. *(Louder murmur from the crowd)*

NADAB: *(Shouting)* Don't be taken in! I sense that you're on the verge of giving in! I'm no prophet, but I can see the future! I see it deep inside me . . . my future . . . is myself. Wherever we go, in all the years to come . . .

MOSES: *(Interrupting him)* Wherever you go, if you are received, you will be unwelcome. People will put up with you, they will tolerate you, until a prince, a priest, or some military leader suddenly takes umbrage at your presence and runs you out of the country amid hatred and bloodshed.

NADAB: But we'll defend ourselves!

MOSES: With what, Nadab?

NADAB: With whatever intelligence, boldness, and courage may dwell within us. We shall work and we shall fight — a weapon in our right hand and a tool in our left. And we'll get rich. We'll get so rich that every time a man, a city or a nation dreams of accomplishing something great, it is to us they will come, from us they will borrow.

MOSES: Rich, yes, but scorned. There will be few men in the world to say sincerely, to dare say that they love you. There will be crowds of them to shout that they despise you. It will be useless for you to be faithful, for you'll wear the mask of treason. The very name of your nation will be an insult. It will not be easy to be a Jew anywhere on earth; you will wear the name of your people like the leprosy.

NADAB: But we'll know how to fight! We'll fight so well, with such valor and skill that all those who relish military prowess and inspired warfare will secretly admire us. For we shall wage wars which will last six days. As we are told that God made the world, we shall make war in six days!

CROWD: *(Unanimous)* In six days!

(Trumpets, very near. The crowd begins to leave the hall slowly.)

MOSES: And the seventh day, all the conquered peoples, all the Arabs that you will have conquered, seated in a circle around you like buzzards watching over the bloody body of a wounded man, will wait until your might has left you, until your attention has been diverted, to pounce on you and cut you to pieces.

NADAB: *(Very slowly following the crowd as it exits)* They'll wait a long time. I'm not uneasy. They'll wait forever.

CROWD: We're not uneasy.

MOSES: Yes, you are uneasy. Physically, I can feel anxiety gnawing away at you. Who would not be uneasy if he groped about like a blind man, pushed, spurred on by the thirst for adventure of impatient youth, but restrained by the faint-hearted caution of old age? So shall you be some day, so you are already — pushed and restrained; smitten by the devouring passion to leave, but hindered by the complacent desire to remain. A nervous people, the most nervous in the world, whose nervousness will be constantly increased, made even more acute by their perception, around them, of the danger of death and total destruction.

NADAB: But one day, one fine day, we will be reassured. Our victory will raise a bulwark around us, and within its shelter we shall live in peace, in a land finally our own, where no one will have the audacity or the strength to drive us away. It is there that we'll create our masterpiece. Listen to me! Listen carefully! Here is the master-work of the Jewish people, having arrived, all told, at the end of our journey.

(The crowd stops an instant.)

CROWD: Listen! Listen!

NADAB: *(Slowly, forcefully)* We shall make, of the desert, a promised land . . .

CROWD: *(With enthusiasm)* Ah!

NADAB: . . . promised to us by us and no longer by the grace of a God who is jealous, and spiteful, and impossible to satisfy. *(He repeats with force.)* We shall make, of the desert . . .

CROWD: . . . a promised land.

NADAB: Let us turn our path toward that land where we shall one day dwell. *(The crowd starts to leave again and begins to sing.)* The water of a great river, controlled by our ingenuity, will irrigate the dry sand which, little by little, will be transformed into fertile land. The grass will sprout up. The trees will grow tall. We'll grow roses, we'll raise oranges and, in the burning atmosphere, beneath a fiery sky, will be heard everywhere as if by a miracle, the sound of flowing water. *(He exits behind the others, but returns immediately.)* For it will be a miracle, a true miracle, without magic or a touch of a wand, a miracle wished for and achieved by man, by a man forced, in order to survive, to be clever and courageous and no longer dependent on this God who is jealous, spiteful, and impossible to satisfy. Let us march toward that miracle, across the sands of time. *(He exits. Moses and Aaron remain on stage. The choral singing grows distant backstage. A short time passes.)*

MOSES: *(To Aaron)* Follow them!

AARON: But . . .

MOSES: *(With feeling)* Follow them, I tell you. Should they need — who can tell? to be supported . . . encouraged in their long and difficult journey, be there, Aaron, be with them and speak to them.

AARON: I don't understand. I thought you said . . .

MOSES: I said so many things that I shouldn't have said. You saw them just as I did. You saw them just now like me. Maybe you also felt yourself pierced . . . penetrated by contradictory feelings. But what remains, Aaron, what remains of all that — the ashes . . . of truth from so many burned words, you must gather. I charge you with that. I'm too old now, to move at their pace, but you, you will catch up with them. Hurry to catch up with them.

AARON: I . . .

MOSES: *(Impatiently)* Come now, go. Hurry!

(Aaron leaves quickly, crosses the stage and exits running. Left alone, Moses hesitates a short while then falls on his knees, facing the audience.) O my God, if ever a man in the world needed You, it's me for sure, right now. Behold me, take me such as I am, in truth and nothing more, as usual, clad in the dignity of being Your servant. I'm nothing but a pitiful old man — lost, misguided, confused, and I don't know which way to turn anymore. That's the truth. I don't understand anything about anything anymore. *(A short pause)* That Nadab — did You see him? — that unbeliever, that rebel, tell me what You think of him, because I must confess that *I* think nothing of him. That's right, Lord, nothing at all. Now he just dragged Your people off with him, did You see him?

I wouldn't have opposed him, that's for sure, but that's not the most serious thing. The most serious, the most disquieting thing is that the desire, even the idea of opposing him didn't even come to me, because everything he said, I admit it to You in secret, everything he said, yelled, and proclaimed seemed to me rather . . . acceptable. When I think that just a month ago, I would have killed him with my own hands! *(A short pause)* Lord, what's happening? What's happening to me? And what's happening to You, whom I hardly recognize? What a change, hm? But who has changed? Is it possible that the whole world has changed that much so rapidly — and the two of us right along with it? Nothing lasts, nothing endures, nothing perseveres. Hardly has anything been born — whatever it may be — when, suddenly, it dies, replaced by something else. Explain this change to me, this great change that I guess, that I *see* taking place in the world and spreading like a forest fire, getting nearer and nearer until everything is in flames. But why must human things resemble ripe fruit, that is shaken by the wind, falls from the tree to the ground, where it rots and is swept away? Where does it . . . where can this gust of world-wide wind come from? *(A short pause)* You saw. You are my witness. The Jewish people have just divorced themselves from me. The people are following their path without me. If need be, they would follow it against me. And against You. They're marching toward a future where we don't count for anything. Neither You. Nor I. All the same, it's astounding.

(A short pause) So, now, what are we going to do? What can we do? What can I do myself? You must, do You hear me, You've got to help me. I can't do anything without You. I've got to feel, as I've felt it so often, Your hand on my shoulder . . . Your heavy, terrible hand on my fragile shoulder and, on the nape of my neck, Your divine breath. I'm waiting, Lord. I'm waiting for Your hand, I'm waiting for Your breath. And then, Your inspiration. All right, Lord, I'm ready. *(He prostrates himself. A rather long*

time passes. Suddenly, he gets up, half-way, with a brusk anxiety.) Why, what a . . . what an impression! What a frightful impression! . . . *(Nervously, he stands up again.)* What a frightful impression of emptiness, above my head! *(In a toneless voice)* To think that the floor of the celestial building, normally inhabited by Your holy presence, now abruptly abandoned, sounds hollow. Everything is hollow, everything is empty. It's like a big house, a . . . palace for rent that nobody rents. It produces the same effect as a vast, vacant room, where nothing makes an echo except the memory of the footsteps that have gone through it. Nobody. There's nobody . . . nobody above me, nobody around me. Everything vanishes. Everything is gone . . . I'm alone . . . I'm alone. *(He begins to pace to the right and to the left, with nervous excitement.)* Where are You? . . . Where is He? . . . Where is the craftsman hiding? *(He stops suddenly in the middle of the stage and, his head held back looking toward the sky, he calls.)* Lord! Lord! *(He lowers his head.)* No answer. He's gone too. Maybe this is, good heavens, a definitive absence. What shall I do? What will become of me? *(A moment of silent meditation)* I suddenly feel as though I'm on another planet, where everything is reversed, things and people, where slaves command and masters obey . . . where the young speak up and the old keep quiet, those good old people who keep quiet while brooding over the false hopes of their ripe old age. Here I am condemned to pretend I accept a great change which I don't even understand. Here I am condemned to drag along behind a nation that, for a long time, I led courageously. I now walk with head down, back bent, and legs weary . . . *(That is the way he begins to walk slowly upstage.)* . . . like one of those more or less crippled laggards who slow down the army. No matter how little you are disposed to laughter, you must find that funny: Moses the pilot, Moses the forerunner, Moses the scout demoted to the rearguard where he moves along so slowly that the people forget him. What path can the pathfinder find now? Ah, sad end to my career! Heartbreaking end to my existence! *(Every ten steps, automatically, because he is in the habit of it and because one can never tell, Moses yells toward the sky. He stops, yells "Lord!", listens three seconds and continues to walk.)* Still nobody, naturally. What a desert! I wonder . . . *(He exits through the door at the rear of the stage, but re-enters immediately.)* I wonder . . . sometimes I wonder whether there was ever anybody up there.
(He exits while the curtain slowly falls.)

The Window

LA FENÊTRE

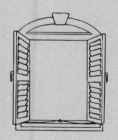

The Window

The scene throughout the play is a bedroom or the second floor of a bakery. Large, but with a low ceiling, the room has one window on the left that looks out on the town square. The window is open. A canopy bed is at upstage right. Between the bed and the left wall an old man, the Grandfather, is asleep in a high-backed tapestry chair. A low stool or two near the chair. A wooden chest under the window. A table with a sprig of flowers in a vase. The floor is red tile.

The room does not occupy the entire stage. Downstage right is a narrow landing with a handrail. The stairway leading downstairs cannot be seen. The door from the bedroom onto the landing is closed when the play begins. As the curtain rises, the Grandfather is in a deep sleep in his chair, in broad daylight. A bright spring sun is shining in at the window.

From the outside rises a muffled noise of people talking and moving about. The clock of a nearby church strikes ten. The Grandfather stirs, mutters something unintelligible and goes back to sleep. As the last strokes of the hour sound, Marie Coutance comes up the stairs, tiptoes across the landing and puts her ear to the bedroom door. She listens.

A GIRL'S VOICE: *(Downstairs)* Mother!
MOTHER: *(With a start)* Shhh! *(She tiptoes back to the head of the stairs.)* Don't make any noise, I think he's asleep. *(She*

goes back and puts her ear against the door. Soon a girl about 20 years old comes up the stairs. She stops on the landing and waits.)

CATHERINE: *(Impatient)* Well, is he?

MOTHER: I don't hear anything.

CATHERINE: So open the door.

MOTHER: It squeaks.

CATHERINE: So what? He'll have to wake up anyway.

MOTHER: Yes, but I want him to sleep as long as he can. He didn't sleep a wink all night, poor man.

CATHERINE: Do you think I don't know? All he did was pace the floor and cough and mumble. It about drove me crazy.

MOTHER: Catherine! He's your grandfather.

CATHERINE: That doesn't give him the right to keep people awake. With the bakery downstairs and Grandfather upstairs, you might as well give up.

MOTHER: It's because he senses that something is happening.

CATHERINE: So why doesn't somebody just tell him once and for all? In the middle of the night he made an enormous racket.

MOTHER: I didn't hear anything.

CATHERINE: I envy the way you can sleep. He must have fallen down.

MOTHER: Fallen down! And you didn't . . .

CATHERINE: He got right back up.

MOTHER: He could have hurt himself! He's blind, Catherine.

CATHERINE: I swear that when he starts pacing that room, you'd never know it. He was charging around like a bull. Shall we go in? *(She reaches out for the doorknob.)*

MOTHER: Wait! Ah, if only he could just sleep until noon. Then everything would be over.

CATHERINE: What about us?

MOTHER: Us?

CATHERINE: Yes, what will we do until noon?

MOTHER: I . . . don't know. We'll stay in the kitchen, in the courtyard, we'll try to . . . to keep busy.

CATHERINE: In the kitchen! But I want to see, Mother! I want to see everything. So does Gilles.

MOTHER: Your father won't want you to.

CATHERINE: Father will be snoring away in the bakehouse the way he does every morning. The morning, as he says, is the baker's night. You could blow off a cannon in his ear. *(She laughs and then speaks again, stubbornly.)* No, Mother, we're going to watch the whole thing. Nobody is going to stop us.

MOTHER: Do you think it'll be a pleasant sight?

CATHERINE: Pleasant or not, we'll see it. Why should we live in a house that looks right out on the square and not . . .

MOTHER: *(Wearily)* You could watch from downstairs.

CATHERINE: The shop is closed. Father told the boys to close the shutters. He's afraid his windows will get broken.

MOTHER: *(Persistent)* You could go up to the attic.

CATHERINE: There's only one little slit of a window! Can't you see us shoving . . .

MOTHER: *(Curtly)* All right, go outside

with the others, the tramps, the street walkers, all the rabble that lives for scandal and blood . . .

CATHERINE: Mother, listen . . .

MOTHER: *(Unmoved)* No. All I ask is that you help me to shield your grandfather, a blind and sick old man, from this . . . violence. Otherwise you can do as you please.

CATHERINE: *(Barely audible)* Yes, Mother.

MOTHER: Thank you, Catherine. *(Pause)* Let's go in now. *(With great care she opens the door and slips cautiously into the room. Catherine follows. They stop. Both speak in whispers until the Grandfather wakes up.)* The door didn't squeak.

CATHERINE: No. It's a wonder it didn't. *(Pause)*

MOTHER: He's asleep.

CATHERINE: What shall we do?

MOTHER: He looks exhausted. *(The noise of the crowd, not too loud yet, comes in through the window.)* Go close the window, Catherine, quietly. Be careful not to wake him.

CATHERINE: Yes, Mother. *(She takes a couple of steps, then turns around.)* Does it squeak too?

MOTHER: I don't know. Wait a minute! Oh, I can't remember. *(The noise of the crowd gets louder.)* We can't help it if it does. Hurry!

(Catherine goes over to the window. She looks out, then draws back almost involuntarily and hurries over to her mother.)

CATHERINE: The square is swarming with people!

MOTHER: Close the window, quick! No, try to pull in the shutters first.

CATHERINE: But . . .

MOTHER: Be quiet! *(Catherine leans out to unfasten the shutters. A woman's shrill laugh suddenly erupts out of the crowd.)* Hurry, child, hurry! *(Catherine closes the shutters, immediately cutting off the ray of light that was shining on the Grandfather. He wakes with a start.)*

GRANDFATHER: What's that? Who's there?

MOTHER: Nothing, Father, it's just us.

GRANDFATHER: Who's "us?"

MOTHER: Catherine and me.

GRANDFATHER: Did you close my shutters?

MOTHER: No, I mean, we . . . we wanted you to be able to sleep. There's a lot of noise outside.

GRANDFATHER: Don't worry about that. I like the sounds of the square, especially on Wednesday.

MOTHER: Why Wednesday?

GRANDFATHER: Because that's market day.

CATHERINE: *(Without thinking)* But there isn't any market today. *(Her mother tries to warn her, but it's too late.)*

GRANDFATHER: No market! *(Catherine silently claps her hand over her mouth, realizing the slip.)* Why not?

MOTHER: Catherine meant . . .

GRANDFATHER: *(Suspicious)* What did she mean?

MOTHER: That they're . . . fixing the square up . . . for . . . for Sunday . . . *(She signals to Catherine to help her.)*

GRANDFATHER: Fixing it up for what?

CATHERINE: For Sunday. It's Pentecost.

GRANDFATHER: So?

CATHERINE: So there's the procession and . . . (She looks desperately at her mother.)

MOTHER: They're putting up . . . poles, you know, for the garlands and banners. They're building a platform for the bishop, the mayor and the municipal officials . . .

GRANDFATHER: (Impatient) They do that every year. They've never called off a market to do it.

MOTHER: Well, they are this year. The municipal council made the decision.

GRANDFATHER: Queer idea. Why didn't somebody tell me?

CATHERINE: Nobody said anything to you?

GRANDFATHER: This is the first I've heard. Did they all vote for it?

MOTHER: I . . . I'm not sure.

CATHERINE: Father will tell you about it. For the moment he's asleep.

MOTHER: Yes, just like every morning. He's sleeping peacefully.

CATHERINE: Like every morning.

GRANDFATHER: I know, I know. (Pause) What's the matter with you?

CATHERINE: Us? Nothing.

MOTHER: Nothing at all. We're just trying to keep you from being upset by . . . by things that . . . that you can't see anymore.

GRANDFATHER: What's got into you? You know it's been years since I've worried about being blind. I see with my ears. Open the shutters!

MOTHER: Father, I . . .

GRANDFATHER: Open them! (Catherine obeys. The sun shines on the old man again.) Ah! That's more like it. (He relaxes.) And they wanted to rob my old face of the warm May sun . . . and this nice breeze that's coming in through my window—the east wind. (Suddenly) Listen! (A sound of hammers pounding heavily on wood) What are they nailing?

MOTHER: Some . . . some plank.

GRANDFATHER: What for?

MOTHER: How should I know?

GRANDFATHER: It must be an impressive plank for a whole crowd of people to gather around it. How many are there?

MOTHER: How many what?

GRANDFATHER: People, down in the square.

MOTHER: I don't know, Father.

GRANDFATHER: Two or three thousand?

MOTHER: (Trying to laugh) Two or three thousand!

GRANDFATHER: I should say so! There's an enormous crowd down there, child!

MOTHER: (Still trying to head him off) Enormous!

GRANDFATHER: Exactly.

CATHERINE: It's a beautiful day, Grandfather! The people are happy to be alive and to be outside. It's May 30, it's almost summer.

MOTHER: Of course, nothing could be simpler.

GRANDFATHER: What kind of plank were they nailing?

CATHERINE: *(Annoyed)* Are you still harping on that plank? Wait a minute. *(She goes over to the window. Her mother watches anxiously.)* It's the top of a sort of . . . of altar.

MOTHER: *(Relieved)* Of course.

GRANDFATHER: What do you mean, "a sort of?" Is it an altar or isn't it?

MOTHER: Listen, Father, you're being difficult. You're getting worked up, you're talking too much. The doctor says you should always get a good night's sleep and even rest part of the day. You're not well.

GRANDFATHER: The doctor doesn't know what he's talking about.

MOTHER: He's been taking care of you for more than twenty years.

GRANDFATHER: I love the sun, the king of doctors. I love the light on my skin and the air of the sky in my nostrils and the sound of the world in my ears. I'll get my fill of sleep soon enough.

MOTHER: But there's just as much sun in our room on the courtyard.

GRANDFATHER: It's *your* room.

MOTHER: Only at night.

GRANDFATHER: It's on the north.

MOTHER: But the air is better than it is here and you have the chestnut tree that's in blossom and it's so quiet . . .

GRANDFATHER: I'll have plenty of quiet when I'm lying next to your poor mother. If I need flowers you'll come put them on my stomach once a week. And the trees of the cemetery — I'll know them down to their roots.

MOTHER: Father!

GRANDFATHER: You annoy me. I'll do as I please. It's my room, in my house. Go away.

MOTHER: You're being unreasonable.

GRANDFATHER: Go on! *(The two women move toward the door.)* If I need you I'll strike the floor with my cane. Until then I want to be alone. *(The women are at the door.)* Are you gone?

MOTHER: No, but we're going.

(They go out and close the door. They look at each other helplessly for a moment on the landing. A woman's voice calls shrilly from downstairs.)

WOMAN'S VOICE: Anybody home?

MOTHER: It's Bertrande. *(Speaking into the stairwell)* Don't shout so, Bertrande.

BERTRANDE: Can I come up?

MOTHER: Not so loud!

BERTRANDE: It's almost time. The half hour just struck.

MOTHER: I'm sorry, Bertrande, but I don't think we can . . . My father isn't feeling well.

BERTRANDE: Oh, really? Poor thing! You're not worried . . . ?

MOTHER: No, no, not for the moment. But after awhile, when he finds out . . .

BERTRANDE: What do you mean, when he finds out? Have you kept it from him?

MOTHER: He gets so upset.

BERTRANDE: But you can't keep him from finding out. His room looks right out on the square. He . . . *(Whatever she intended to say is drowned out by the Grandfather's voice.)*

GRANDFATHER: Oh! What are those women chattering about now? *(Pause. He* gets up.) Are you finished? *(With the help of his cane, he starts over to the door.)*

MOTHER: Come on, quick! Let's go downstairs. *(The women hurry away. Pause. The Grandfather opens the door, listens a moment and then slams the door violently.)*

GRANDFATHER: What in the world's got into them? *(He remains immobile, leaning on his cane. His head is inclined slightly forward as it usually is when he is listening carefully. After awhile, he goes over to the window. He listens.)* There must be ten, twelve thousand people down there. *(Noise of the crowd increases.)* Maybe more, fifteen thousand, waiting for . . . What are they waiting for? *(He listens.)* Something has been going on for two days. They say it hasn't, but they won't tell me. Something . . . something strange. *(The first note of a knell, very slow, very sonorous; the Grandfather listens intently.)* What's that? The death-knell? *(Murmurs from the crowd. The Grandfather waits, tense. The second note sounds.)* The knell, that's it. Then there must be a funeral. Who died? *(Third note. The crowd gets louder.)* It must be somebody important, a prince or a bishop. Could it be the old bishop? No, it's not him. My daughter told me they were putting up a platform for him in the square. Although what Marie says lately is not as important as what she doesn't say. But why would she not tell me about the death of a bishop? Or a prince? *(The knell sounds again.)* I've got to know! *(He turns toward the door and shouts.)* Hey, you women! *(He raises his cane as if to strike the floor, but*

the sound of the hammer interrupts him.)* There's that infernal hammer again! *(He listens intently. The hammer and the knell resound above the noise of the crowd. A little boy and girl, François and Berthe, come scampering up the stairs to the landing. Like two mice, they scurry over to the door and listen in silence. They talk in very audible children's whispers until the Grandfather opens the door.)*

BERTHE: He's not moving.

FRANÇOIS: No, he's asleep. Should we go in?

BERTHE: But what if he's not asleep?

FRANÇOIS: We'll run away. He won't know who it is since he can't see.

BERTHE: We think he can't see, but he knows everything that goes on.

FRANÇOIS: Come on, let's go in.

BERTHE: Watch out.

FRANÇOIS: I can do it. *(He opens the door which squeaks, naturally. The Grandfather, in a single movement, wheels around to face the children and thunders at them.)*

GRANDFATHER: Who's there? *(No answer)* Answer me!

BERTHE: *(Terrified)* It's us, Grandfather.

GRANDFATHER: Berthe and François?

FRANÇOIS: *(His voice quavering)* Yes, Grandfather. We thought you were . . .

GRANDFATHER: *(Interrupting)* Well, I wasn't. Come here. *(Trembling almost visibly, the children join their grandfather at the window. Pause. Noise from the crowd.)* Tell me what's happening outside.

FRANÇOIS: *(Too quickly)* Nothing, Grandfather.

BERTHE: *(Almost interrupting François)* Nothing at all.

GRANDFATHER: Be careful what you say. You know where dirty little liars end up? In hell! In the fire! Roasted like chickens! *(Silence. The hammer sounds again.)* What's that man nailing with the hammer?

FRANCOIS: It's nothing, Grandfather, he's putting up a notice.

GRANDFATHER: A notice?

BERTHE: Yes, at the top of a pole, very high up.

FRANCOIS: It's nothing. Don't worry. *(Silence)* We have to go now. Mother wouldn't want us to bother you. *(He signals to his sister.)*

GRANDFATHER: *(His voice changed)* Where is the pole?

BERTHE: In the square.

GRANDFATHER: But where?

FRANCOIS: In the middle of a platform. We have to go, Grandfather.

GRANDFATHER: What kind of platform?

BERTHE: We don't know. Mother will spank us . . .

GRANDFATHER: *(Angry)* Would you rather I'd do it? So what is it? What kind of platform? Are you going to answer me? *(He raises his cane.)*

BERTHE: *(Crying)* It's not even a platform, it's just logs.

GRANDFATHER: Logs?

BERTHE: Yes, big logs.

FRANCOIS: It's true. And kindling.

GRANDFATHER: Kindling! *(To himself)* The bastards. *(He goes over to his chair and sits down heavily. Pause. He straightens up. His old hands grip the arms of the chair ferociously. He is overcome by a cold anger. The children have gone over to the window and are looking out, fascinated.)*

VOICE OF THEIR MOTHER: *(Downstairs)* Where are they? *(The children jump. The voice is nearer now.)* Where are they? *(The children try to escape, but they are trapped. Their mother is coming up the stairs.)* I'll bet I know where they are. *(She comes in.)*

MOTHER: Of course you're here, where else? *(She rushes at the children and grabs them.)* You little devils! Monsters! *(She swats at them ineffectively.)*

FRANCOIS: We didn't say anything, Mama. Did we, Grandfather?

GRANDFATHER: *(Faraway)* Nothing, nothing . . .

BERTHE: All I said was there were logs.

FRANCOIS: I said there was kindling. Nothing else.

BERTHE: Oh, François, we told about the notice too.

FRANCOIS: The notice and the pole, but that's all.

MOTHER: Get out! *(She makes a vaguely threatening gesture. The children scramble to the door.)*

FRANCOIS: *(On the way out)* I even told Grandfather not to worry. Didn't I, Grandfather?

MOTHER: Go on! *(She starts toward them. They clatter down the stairs. Pause. The Mother walks slowly over to the Grandfather's left, between him and the window. Silence.)*

GRANDFATHER: Why did you tell me that that poor girl was saved?

MOTHER: But Father, she was when I saw her on Thursday . . .

GRANDFATHER: (Interrupting her) You saw her!

MOTHER: Yes, Thursday, when she was coming back from Saint-Ouen.

GRANDFATHER: You hide everything from me.

MOTHER: Everything I can, Father, yes. It's too sad a story. (Pause)

GRANDFATHER: And you saw her! What's she like?

MOTHER: A tall girl, very pretty, dark hair . . .

GRANDFATHER: (Interrupting again) Dark? I would have thought she was blonde.

MOTHER: No, her hair is brown. She was crying.

GRANDFATHER: The things they did to her. And we don't know everything. She was crying?

MOTHER: Like a fountain. The tears were rolling down her cheeks.

GRANDFATHER: She didn't try to hide them?

MOTHER: How could she? Her hands were bound by a coarse rope and tied to the rail of the cart.

GRANDFATHER: They put her in a cart?

MOTHER: It's a long way from the cemetery at Saint-Ouen. (Pause) Her eyes are very light.

(Sudden outburst from the square — shouts, insults, oaths)

GRANDFATHER: (Jerking himself around to face the window) What's going on?

MOTHER: (Turning toward the window) Nothing, it's just the soldiers. They're moving people back with pitchfork handles.

GRANDFATHER: Soldiers! (He spits on the floor.) They have to do their duty. But all those others, those scum that came to gawk! (He gets up.) Shame on this wretched city! (He takes a step toward the window.)

MOTHER: Father! (She steps between him and the window.) Be careful! (She makes him sit down.) There are spies everywhere!

GRANDFATHER: The city of Rouen is about to lose its honor. (Another outburst from the crowd) Listen to them! (After a few moments the noise recedes.) Tell me the truth, Marie, last Thursday when you saw her in the cart, did you really think she was saved?

MOTHER: I did, I told you I did. She had . . . She had — what's the word? — she had abjured.

GRANDFATHER: What does "abjure" mean? That she swore she lied?

MOTHER: I think so.

GRANDFATHER: She wouldn't do it.

MOTHER: They say she did.

GRANDFATHER: Then they're lying.

MOTHER: Probably they are, but they're stronger. According to them, she admitted that everything she said in court, everything—her visions, her voices, her mission, the voices, you know, that came to her out of the sky, from St. Michae and St. Catherine — all that was made up.

GRANDFATHER: But you didn t tell me that. You just told me they pardoned her.

100

MOTHER: I didn't dare say anything. I knew they'd figure out a way to trick her. And they did. On Friday morning she put her men's clothes back on.

GRANDFATHER: Because they had forbidden her to?

MOTHER: Yes, it seems they're diabolical or something.

GRANDFATHER: That's absurd!

MOTHER: I know.

GRANDFATHER: What if she didn't have any other clothes in prison?

MOTHER: Try to prove that!

GRANDFATHER: I know, but what God damned nonsense! As if heaven or hell were a question of skirts or breeches. None of this makes any sense.

MOTHER: It makes too much sense. She frightens the English. They trumped up charges against her. And since they couldn't take her in battle, they . . . well, they bought her.

GRANDFATHER: And the loyal Burgundians sold her. If I knew the bastard . . . *(Silence. Noises from the square.)* How old is she?

MOTHER: Nineteen.

GRANDFATHER: Catherine's age.

MOTHER: Yes.

GRANDFATHER: Can you imagine, Marie! A girl like Catherine, tied to a stake, facing the crowd, on top of a pile of firewood!

MOTHER: Don't say that, Father!

GRANDFATHER: Can you imagine! *(Silence)* Where did they put the . . . thing?

MOTHER: In the middle of the square. Facing Holy Savior Church. *(Pause. The church clock strikes the hour.)*

GRANDFATHER: What time is it?

MOTHER: Eleven o'clock.

GRANDFATHER: Is that the time they picked? *(A muffled drumbeat makes the answer unnecessary.)* At least they're prompt. *(The drums get slightly louder.)*

MOTHER: Let me close the window.

GRANDFATHER: No, I want to be there. *(The drums are still louder. Someone is coming up the stairs, talking excitedly.)* Who's that on the stairs?

MOTHER: Catherine and a neighbor.

GRANDFATHER: Which neighbor?

MOTHER: Bertrande.

GRANDFATHER: The carpenter's wife?

MOTHER: Yes, Bertrande Maillard. I'll tell them that you . . . *(She starts toward the door.)*

GRANDFATHER: *(Interrupting her)* No, let them come in. It'll be good for them to see it.

(Catherine and Bertrande appear on the landing, then Bertrande's husband, Etienne.)

MOTHER: I'm afraid they'll upset you. Catherine is young and thoughtless. She thinks she's tough-skinned. Bertrande's husband works for the English . . .

GRANDFATHER: *(Finishing her sentence)* And eats French bread. *(Catherine, Bertrande, and Etienne enter.)*

BERTRANDE: Hello, Monsieur Thibaut. How are you?

GRANDFATHER: Fine, neighbor, fine. But that's just a manner of speaking. Nothing is fine today.

ETIENNE: No, the times are bad.

GRANDFATHER: Ah! Is it the carpenter?

ETIENNE: Hello, Monsieur Thibaut.

BERTRANDE: I didn't think you'd mind if I brought him along.

GRANDFATHER: It's not the times that are bad, neighbor, it's the people.

ETIENNE: That's a fact.

MOTHER: (Aside to Catherine) What are the children doing?

CATHERINE: (Aside to her mother) I locked them up in the kitchen. (During this short scene, the drum rolls have become slightly louder. Then they stop. Everyone except the Grandfather turns toward the window. In the distance a Latin chant begins, sung by men's voices.)

GRANDFATHER: Is that the penitents?

MOTHER: (Aside to the Grandfather) Yes, the white penitents. (The chant comes closer.)

GRANDFATHER: I can just see them under their cowls. Arms crossed and stuck in their sleeves. Two holes for their eyes in their white hoods. Is that right?

MOTHER: (Aside to Grandfather) Yes, Father.

(The chant comes still closer.)

GRANDFATHER: Whose penitence are they working on? Hmm? I'm asking you. For whom are these penitents parading?

BERTRANDE: For the girl, Monsieur Thibaut.

GRANDFATHER: That's what I suspected. But the girl, as you say, Madame Maillard, the poor girl has penitence enough for all of them.

ETIENNE: They say that she . . .

GRANDFATHER: (Interrupting him) They can say whatever they want. She has penitence to spare for the whole city of Rouen! And for all Normandy! And for the whole wretched kingdom of France! And they can use it, believe me!

ETIENNE: There isn't any more kingdom of France, you know perfectly well.

GRANDFATHER: (Rising abruptly) No more kingdom . . .

MOTHER: (Interrupting him) Father! You promised me you'd not get upset.

GRANDFATHER: I can't let that pass . . .

MOTHER: (Interrupting again) You can, and so can Maillard. Whether you love or hate the girl, you must respect her death. (Pause)

GRANDFATHER: You're right, Marie. (He sits down. The chant is closer now.) But I'm sure, you hear me? I'm certain that in her simple way, in her innocence of flesh and spirit, this girl is like a . . . a vessel filled with milk. (To himself) Yes, pure white milk. (The chant is just outside the window.) Poor little white penitent . . . (The chanters pass by under the window. Silence in the room. François appears silently on the landing. He turns back to signal to someone on the stairs.)

FRANÇOIS: (Whispering) Watch out! They left the door open! (Gilles, François' older brother, about 20 years old, appears, followed by Berthe. They all speak in stage whispers until they enter the room. François is wild with excitement.) Come on! Gilles goes first and then us! Hurry up! (Unable to contain himself, he dances up and down.)

GILLES: Don't jump around that way. It's not a country fair.

FRANÇOIS: But it's exciting!

GILLES: You think so?

FRANÇOIS: Don't you? She's nothing but a dirty girl.

GILLES: Do you know her?

BERTHE: They told us she was. And she's a witch too! When she gets on a horse, the devil hops on and rides behind her!

GILLES: Did you see them?

BERTHE: Cabott saw them.

GILLES: Who's Cabott?

BERTHE: The Englishman that stays with the Maillards. He saw them more than ten times.

GILLES: Does he have eyes in the back of his head?

FRANÇOIS: No, why?

GILLES: Because every time she rode up on her horse, Cabott and his crew turned tail and ran.

FRANÇOIS: Did you see them?

GILLES: No, but I wish I had. Come on, let's go in. And you behave or I'll swat you like flies and put you back in the kitchen. *(They enter, first Gilles and then the children who immediately run over and climb onto the box under the window. Pantomime between Catherine and the Mother who do not agree on what should be done about the children. François and Berthe promise by gestures that they will be good. Silence)*

GRANDFATHER: *(Suddenly)* Did Gilles just come in?

GILLES: Yes, Grandfather. Hello.

ETIENNE: *(To the Grandfather)* How the devil can you tell who it is?

GRANDFATHER: Gilles smells like fresh, warm bread. *(To Gilles)* How did your work go today, boy?

GILLES: The chimney wouldn't draw right. There's an east wind.

GRANDFATHER: I know. It started around midnight.

GILLES: And then we had to bake almost twice as much as usual.

GRANDFATHER: What for?

GILLES: Father thought we'd have to feed all those people. *(He makes a gesture toward the square.)* They'll be hungry afterwards.

GRANDFATHER: Yes, the beasts, and thirsty.

GILLES: They've come from everywhere — Sotteville, Maromme, Bois-Guillaume, Darnétal — everywhere, even Jumièges. It's a regular army.

GRANDFATHER: If it were an army, it'd be smaller. *(Turning abruptly to the window)* Filthy cowards!

ETIENNE: Why cowards? The people are tired of war, Monsieur Thibaut, it's as simple as that.

GRANDFATHER: The people, Monsieur Maillard, are tired of everything, and it's not as simple as that. They were born tired, loveless, faithless and cowardly.

ETIENNE: It's because they've been told for centuries that they're nothing. They've ended up believing it. The king's war isn't their war, Monsieur Thibaut.

MOTHER: Please, Father, Monsieur Maillard . . .

GRANDFATHER: There's one thing on earth, Monsieur Maillard, that's greater than the king, and that's the land. It's worth fighting for.

ETIENNE: There's something even greater than the land, Monsieur Thibaut, and that's life. People's lives are too short to be spent in a war that lasts a hundred years.

MOTHER: Please, Monsieur Maillard, Father . . .

GRANDFATHER: In '76, Monsieur Maillard, I was young and I loved life. I was 20 years old and I hung onto life by every fiber of body and soul. And do you know what I did, in September '76, almost on my 21st birthday? In this square where you're looking right now, I saw Bertrand Du Guesclin ride by on his horse, headed for Gévaudon. I followed him. And what was Gévaudon to me? I'm asking you. What was Gévaudon with its rocks and its skinny sheep to a son of our beautiful green Normandy?

ETIENNE: In those days . . .

GRANDFATHER: (Interrupting him) No, answer me! And what was the city of Orleans? What were Jargeau and Beaugency? What were the court of Bourges and its sleepy little king? What was the cathedral of Reims, far away like a dream in the clouds, to this poor girl from Lorraine, who is 20 years old, just as I was, who was born of humble parents, this girl that nobody followed? You have no idea, Monsieur Maillard . . .

FRANÇOIS: (Exploding with excitement) There she is!

BERTHE: (Shrilly) I see her too!
(The crowd roars.)

FRANÇOIS: She's on a wagon! She has on a yellow dress!

BERTHE: It's not a dress, it's a shirt, a yellow shirt!

FRANCOIS: Let me tell it, let me tell it! She has on a tall hat . . .

BERTHE: (Interrupting him) Yes, a pointed hat . . .

FRANÇOIS: (Interrupting her) Like a bishop's hat. And there are lots of soldiers on the wagon!

GRANDFATHER: (Angry) That's enough! (Silence in the room. Like an icy wind invading the May morning, the strains of De Profundis begin in the distance.) What are these two chatterboxes doing here?

CATHERINE: I locked them up . . .

GILLES: I let them out, Grandfather, but I'll take them away for you. (To the children) Come on, you brats! Downstairs!

GRANDFATHER: No, let them stay. It'll be their punishment. (Silence. The chanters advance slowly. The Grandfather speaks softly.) How does she look? Is she afraid?

CATHERINE: She's too far away, Grandfather. The procession is going all around the square.

GRANDFATHER: Naturally! They're prolonging the pleasure! (Pause)

CATHERINE: (Suddenly, in a dull voice) Oh, it's terrible, I . . . I . . . it's terrible . . .

GRANDFATHER: What is it, Cathy?

CATHERINE: I don't know. My heart is racing . . . I . . .

MOTHER: *(Gently)* Go to your room.

CATHERINE: No, I can't. *(Long pause. The chanters are nearer.)*

GRANDFATHER: *(Bitter)* More penitents?

MOTHER: Yes. These are dressed in red.

GRANDFATHER: That hardly makes them festive, if memory serves.

MOTHER: They're sinister.

BERTRANDE: You can say that again. *(Pause Chant)*

GRANDFATHER: What are they doing now?

MOTHER: They're walking in front of the wagon.

GRANDFATHER: Where are the soldiers?

MOTHER: Behind.

(Pause. Chant)

ETIENNE: It's been a long time since they've been around.

GRANDFATHER: Who? The soldiers?

ETIENNE: No, the red penitents.

GRANDFATHER: Ah, them . . . because the soldiers have been around plenty long. That's about all there *has* been around here lately *(Aggressive)* Isn't that right?

ETIENNE: *(Conciliatory)* Yes, Monsieur Thibaut, that's right.

GRANDFATHER: When I think that if I'd been lucky I could have lost my eyes before!

BERTRANDE: Before what, Monsieur Thibaut?

GRANDFATHER: Before seeing the English, Madame Maillard! *(Angry)* Before they poisoned the air of Normandy! Before

their filthy faces became a part of the landscape of our poor country!

MOTHER: *(Anxious)* Father. Father, please!

GRANDFATHER: I don't care, let them burn me! Let them burn me with her! I'll never find a better way to die!

ETIENNE: That's what they say.

GRANDFATHER: And they'd do it!

CATHERINE: *(Obviously suffering)* Please don't talk about it.

(The chant approaches. Pause)

FRANÇOIS: Here she comes! Look, look! She's going to pass right by our window!

BERTHE: She's not tied up, did you notice? Maybe she'll get away!

FRANÇOIS: Get away? I'd like to see that! With all those soldiers?

BERTHE: I'd try it if I were . . .

CATHERINE: *(Interrupting her)* Don't talk about it! Make them be quiet, Mother. Please make them be quiet.

MOTHER: *(Tenderly)* Yes, my child. *(To the children)* One more word and down the stairs you go.

GILLES: *(With a threatening gesture toward the children)* Head first.

FRANÇOIS: Grandfather said we could stay.

GILLES: But with your mouths shut. *(To Catherine, gently)* What's the matter, Catherine?

CATHERINE: *(Stammering)* Oh, Gilles, I don't know, I . . . It's like a flood of tears, welled up inside me, a torrent of . . . of . . . I feel shaky . . .

GILLES: Come lean on me. *(He puts his*

105

arm around her.)

BERTRANDE: How sensitive she is!

GILLES: Yes, she is. *(To Catherine)* It's all right, old girl.

(The chant is quite near. Soon it will pass by the window. The following lines are spoken in between phrases of the chant and must be almost shouted in order to be audible.)

GILLES: Shall I close the window, Grandfather?

GRANDFATHER: *(Sitting rigidly in his chair)* No! Let it tear us apart!

GILLES: *(To Catherine)* Come with me, Catherine.

CATHERINE: *(Distracted)* Where? Where?

GILLES: I don't know. In the back, in the courtyard . . .

CATHERINE: I have to stay here.

GRANDFATHER: Let it tear us apart and make us bleed!

(The chant passes under the window and for a moment drowns out all other sounds. Pause. Then Catherine speaks abruptly, in a piercing voice.)

CATHERINE: My God, she's looking at me! Can't you see? She's looking right at me. *(She draws back, as if someone had struck her, and puts her hands over her eyes..Then she rushes to the window and cries out plaintively.)* Joan! Joan!

BERTRANDE: *(Horrified)* Good lord, get back in here! *(She snatches at Catherine's clothes and attempts to drag her back from the window.)*

ETIENNE: You better watch that, Catherine. It's dangerous.

CATHERINE: *(Like a trapped animal)* My

God, what can I do? What can I do? *(She looks desperately around the room. Suddenly she runs to the table, grabs the flowers out of the vase, returns to the window and in an almost savage gesture of love, throws them into the square.)*

MOTHER: *(Crying out)* Catherine!

GILLES: Oh!

BERTRANDE: *(Furious)* She's crazy! She'll get us all hanged!

FRANÇOIS: *(Bursts out laughing)* Ha ha! A soldier got them right in the face!

BERTHE: Ha ha! He jerked back and almost lost his helmet!

ETIENNE: *(Frightened)* Is he angry?

FRANÇOIS: No, he thinks they were for him!

BERTHE: "Thank you," he said, "Thank you!"

ETIENNE: Thank God! *(He wipes his forehead.)*

BERTRANDE: Or somebody! *(To Catherine)* What got into you?

CATHERINE: *(As if in great pain)* Oh, Grandfather, Grandfather! *(She throws herself at his feet. Sobs rack her body. The old man tenderly strokes her hair while the chant moves away.)*

MOTHER: My poor child. *(She kneels beside Catherine.)* I told you it would be terrible.

GRANDFATHER: *(Quietly)* What did she do, exactly?

GILLES: *(Not without pride)* She threw her your flowers.

BERTRANDE: Flowers! Can you believe it?

GRANDFATHER: What a good idea!

ETIENNE: Are you serious?

GRANDFATHER: What a wonderful idea!

BERTRANDE: Another one like that and none of us will be around to have any more!

CATHERINE: *(Raising her head)* She looked at me. She looked at me so sweetly . . . *(She begins to cry again.)*

MOTHER: Now, now, Catherine. *(She puts her arm around Catherine. Silence in the room as the chant fades.)*

CATHERINE: *(Disengaging herself)* Suddenly she looked right into my eyes with an expression so sweet . . .

GRANDFATHER: *(Quietly)* She won't be afraid.

CATHERINE: *(Wanting to be convinced)* She won't? You really don't think so? *(She jumps up, suddenly revived.)*

GRANDFATHER: I know she won't.

CATHERINE: She must feel alone — hideously alone. *(Silence. Everyone looks down.)*

FRANÇOIS: Here it comes! She's getting down from the wagon!

(Again all attention is turned to the window.)

BERTHE: There's a monk with her, all in white!

FRANÇOIS: He is not!

BERTHE: He is too!

FRANÇOIS: No, he's not! He has on a black coat!

BERTHE: But his habit's white!

GILLES: That's enough, you two! *(To the others)* It's a Dominican. *(He goes over to the window.)* He's young.

GRANDFATHER: Good! Old monks don't have any heart left.

MOTHER: Oh, Father!

GRANDFATHER: It's true. Their soul crowds it out.

GILLES: *(At the window)* He's holding her by the arm. He's as pale as a ghost.

FRANÇOIS: Are they going to burn him too?

GILLES: *(Stern)* Don't be funny!

GRANDFATHER: He's not being funny. He thinks it'd be perfectly normal if they did. It's a sad world where nothing astonishes a child.

GILLES: They're crossing the square together . . . The sun is bright . . . It's strange to see . . . *(Suddenly alert)* Hey, what's that?

CATHERINE: What is it? *(Instinctive movement toward the window)*

MOTHER: *(Holding her back)* Stay here!

GILLES: A gust of wind knocked off the hat she's wearing—you know, the mitre . . .

GRANDFATHER: *(Impatient)* Then what happened?

GILLES: One of the soldiers bent down to pick it up, but just at that moment the Dominican stepped on it and crushed it.

FRANÇOIS: *(Laughing)* Flat as a pancake!

BERTHE: The soldier's mad!

GILLES: Now they're stopping at the stage.

GRANDFATHER: The stage? Is there a stage?

GILLES: Yes, Grandfather. It's draped in purple and swarming with churchmen and English officers.

GRANDFATHER: You didn't tell me that!

MOTHER: What does it matter, Father?

GRANDFATHER: Everything matters! Was that your "altar," Catherine?

CATHERINE: Yes, Grandfather.

GRANDFATHER: You could have found a less noble word for a pig sty.

BERTRANDE: Monsieur Thibaut!

GRANDFATHER: *(Raising his voice)* Pigs! Gilles, see if you can make out their faces! Are there any local breeds? The mayor? The judge? Some miserable boot-licker? Who do you see?

(The Mother makes a sign to Gilles not to answer.)

GILLES: The stage is at an angle from here. The sun is in my eyes. *(Suddenly alert again)* What does *he* want?

CATHERINE: *(Immediately)* Who?

GILLES: One of the men on the stage. He's going over to the edge.

CATHERINE: What kind of man?

GILLES: A priest. He's going to say something.

GRANDFATHER: Say something! Fine time for that!

GILLES: He's pushing back his sleeves . . . making the sign of the cross . . . he's going to give a sermon!

GRANDFATHER: Another quarter of an hour! *(Pause)*

MOTHER: Poor child!

BERTRANDE: Yes, how thoughtless.

CATHERINE: Thoughtless? It's inhuman!

GRANDFATHER: It's all part of the game. They have to drag it out. What's he saying?

GILLES: I can't hear.

CATHERINE: What about her? What's she doing?

GILLES: Standing straight as a tree. The good Dominican is trembling beside her. But she hasn't flinched. She's a soldier!

GRANDFATHER: *(Echoing Gilles)* A soldier. *(Silence. A man about 38 years old appears on the landing. He is tired. He knocks softly at the door.)* Who's there? Come in! *(The man enters.)*

MOTHER: Ah, it's you, Audouin!

AUDOUIN: Yes, cousin, good morning. Hello, Uncle Thibaut.

GRANDFATHER: Hello, Audouin. What brings you here?

AUDOUIN: May I sit down? My legs are about to give out. *(He sits down wearily on a stool.)*

GRANDFATHER: Been walking all that much?

AUDOUIN: No, no, it's not that. You ask what brings me here. You're going to laugh, but . . . *(He hesitates.)*

GRANDFATHER: Go on. It'll be a change.

AUDOUIN: I came to sell a cow.

ETIENNE: A cow? Today?

AUDOUIN: Isn't this market day?

GRANDFATHER: No market today. The square is occupied.

AUDOUIN: I see that now. Only I hadn't known a thing about it. You city folks find out all the news, but Malaunay's like the end of the world. When I left the village around 6 o'clock this morning, I was alone on the road, all alone in my cart with my horse in front and the cow behind. If any-body had told me what I'd find when I got here . . .

FRANÇOIS: Which cow is it?

AUDOUIN: Rosie.

BERTHE: Oh, good old Rosie! You promised her to me!

AUDOUIN: I'll give you another one. Besides, good old Rosie may not be so good anymore. I've got to make her go all the way back home after she's just run halfway here. She'll probably lose ten pounds.

GRANDFATHER: You don't drive her very fast, do you?

AUDOUIN: I don't drive her at all. It's Captain.

GRANDFATHER: Captain who?

FRANÇOIS: His horse.

AUDOUIN: That damned old plug! When it's just the two of us, me in the cart and him in the harness, I have to wear out my arm and his flanks to get him to put one foot in front of the other. But the minute I tie a cow onto the back of the cart, he's off to the races.

(Everyone laughs.)

GRANDFATHER: You think he does it on purpose?

AUDOUIN: You bet I do! He's the meanest son-of-a-bitch I know!

(More laughing)

GRANDFATHER: Where are they?

AUDOUIN: Who?

GRANDFATHER: All three of them — your horse, your cow, and your cart.

AUDOUIN: In a corner of the courtyard at the Old Apple Tree cafe, in the shade. I had the devil of a time finding somewhere to leave them. You ought to see all the people in this town! And the racket they make! The place is crawling with kettles and tubs of food, sides of beef roasting on spits, ducks being dressed, serving girls by the drove! It's like a fair!

MOTHER: It's a disgrace.

AUDOUIN: And I didn't know a thing about it!

ETIENNE: Oh, come now!

AUDOUIN: I swear I didn't. After I passed through Maromme and got to the main road where all those people were headed for Rouen, I thought it was a little odd, I admit. But it was market day and the weather was perfect which doesn't happen very often around here. So I just supposed everybody was out because of the sun and I figured I'd be sure to find a buyer for Rosie. We sort of washed into town like a big happy wave, hundreds of us.

ETIENNE: Weren't the people talking on the way to town?

AUDOUIN: Aw, you know how people are, especially country people. They talk about everything but what's bothering them. I swear I had no idea what was going on until I got to the Saint-Maclou gate and that was a little late to turn back, wasn't it? There was one of those Goddams at the gate, a bowman. He saw somebody he knew in the crowd, a big fat farmer from Maromme, and he yelled out to him, "Bonjure, bonjure! They're roasting the queen pig today!"

GRANDFATHER: *(Jumping up from his chair)* Good God! And you still didn't . . .

AUDOUIN: At first I didn't catch on . . .

GRANDFATHER: I'd have made him eat his bow!

ETIENNE: *(Quietly) Oh, no.*

GRANDFATHER: And his quiver!

AUDOUIN: Suddenly everything fell into place. I saw the whole thing, I understood what those people meant on the road by their winks and grunts and silences. My head started ringing like a bell, and I thought I must be seeing things. I felt so wretched just sitting there doing nothing that I stumbled out of my cart and walked the rest of the way beside my horse. *(Silence. Audouin's voice betrays genuine emotion.)* Just imagine, I didn't even know they had convicted her. *(Silence)* At home everybody loved that girl. We had her portrait over our fireplace. We called her Little Joan.

CATHERiNE: Her portrait?

AUDOUIN: The spit and image. One of her comrades who fought with her at Jardeau happened to stop by our place on his way home to Picardy. He was on crutches, poor boy. We put him up for the night, and he did her portrait for us.

BERTRANDE: So he was a painter?

AUDOUIN: No, a soldier, and a good one. But he had a knack of creating life with whatever he could get his hands on. This time it was a hunk of charcoal he fished out of the fireplace' after dinner. He started drawing on the wall above the mantle and in a few minutes there she was with her helmet and her short hair and . . . her smile.

BERTRANDE: You sound like you're in love with her!

AUDOUIN: Don't be ridiculous! No, she was . . . how can I explain it . . . the protector of our home, a sort of . . . of angel, stronger than the evil in the world,

sweeter than everyday life. A Sunday angel. We always looked at her when we went by and it was easier to live . . . *(Pause)* When we found out she had been captured at Compiègne, my wife and I weren't scared for a minute. We were sure she'd get away. *(Silence)*

GRANDFATHER: How is she?

AUDOUIN: Who?

GRANDFATHER: Your wife.

AUDOUIN: She was fine. *(Pause)* I'll have to put a piece of glass up to protect the portrait. A charcoal drawing won't last very long. *(Pause)*

CATHERINE: May I go see the portrait?

AUDOUIN: Whenever you want to, Catherine. *(Pause)*

CATHERINE: Could I go home with you today, Audouin?

MOTHER: Catherine!

CATHERINE: Yes, Mother, to Malaunay. I can't stay here tonight.

MOTHER: Of course you can.

CATHERINE: No, I can't.

BERTRANDE: How sensitive she is!

AUDOUIN: We'll leave in my cart at sundown, when all these people have gone home. We won't talk much. We'll see the full moon rise.

MOTHER: She'll have to ask her father's . . .

GRANDFATHER: *(Interrupting her)* I'll answer for him.

CATHERINE: *(Suddenly coming alive)* Oh, thank you, Grandfather, thank you!

BERTRANDE: She must really like portraits.

ETIENNE: I hope it at least looks like her.

110

AUDOUIN: How should I know if it does or doesn't? I never saw her in my life.

ETIENNE: Well, look at her.

FRANÇOIS: He can't see anything. She's got her back turned.

AUDOUIN: I don't need to see her, I know it's her. I'm positive. I can feel it.

BERTRANDE: The eyes of faith, in other words.

GILLES: *(Suddenly, from the window)* She's turning around, come here! She's turning this way!

AUDOLIN: She's turning around . . .

GILLES: Come see her!

AUDOUIN: I don't dare.

GILLES: Hurry! Come look at her!

(Audouin runs to the window. Pause)

AUDOUIN: That's her. I knew it would be.

CATHERINE: Oh, God! I'd forgotten she still has to die!

AUDOUIN: I recognize her, that's her.

BERTRANDE: You have good eyesight.

AUDOJIN: I see her! I see her!

GRANDFATHER: What's she doing?

AUDOUIN: I see her.

GILLES: Her confessor is whispering something to her.

GRANDFATHER: What about the priest? Is he still talking?

GILLES: No, he's finished. He's wiping his forehead.

GRANDFATHER: I'll bet he is. What a job he has!

ETIENNE: He may be sincere.

GRANDFATHER: Why not? You are.

BERTRANDE: Exactly. What do you take us for, Monsieur Thibaut? Do you think we enjoy seeing that poor girl burned alive?

It's true we don't care for her, but that's a far cry from . . .

GRANDFATHER: *(Interrupting her)* She's going to die for you.

BERTRANDE: Don't be absurd.

GRANDFATHER: For you!

BERTRANDE: I'm hardly asking her to do that!

GRANDFATHER: She's going to show the world that a people it takes for dead is not even afraid of death!

BERTRANDE: The world couldn't care less.

GRANDFATHER: She actually believes that!

BERTRANDE: The world, Monsieur Thibaut, has other concerns.

GRANDFATHER: What concerns, Madame Maillard?

BERTRANDE: Bread to eat, money to spend, and a bed to make love in.

ETIENNE: Bertrande!

MOTHER: Madame Maillard!

BERTRANDE: *(Violently)* Let's say what we mean and quit beating around the bush! If Joan of Lorraine had minded her own business . . .

GRANDFATHER: *(Interrupting her)* Instead of being prisoners, we'd be slaves!

BERTRANDE: More big words! Maybe we *would* be slaves, but we'd have peace.

GRANDFATHER: *(Exasperated)* What kind of woman is this, anyway? Peace, you poor fool . . .

ETIENNE: *(Interrupting him)* Hey, hey, take it easy. We can say what we think without scratching each other's eyes out.

GRANDFATHER: Nobody can stop me from . . .

(A deep bell sounds once, like a stone falling.)

AUDOUIN : Oh! She's kneeling. *(Pause)*

CATHERINE: Kneeling? Where?

GILLES: On the ground.

CATHERINE: On the cobblestones!

GILLES: Yes, in the middle of the square. Come over here and see her.

CATHERINE: It hurts too much.

GILLES: Come see her, Catherine! She's all alone and stronger than this whole rotten crowd put together! She's beautiful, Catherine, come see her!

CATHERINE: No, I couldn't stand it. *(She hides her face in her hands. Pause)*

FRANÇOIS: Why did they put that yellow dress on her, Mama?

BERTHE: It's not a dress, it's a shirt.

FRANÇOIS: I mean that yellow shirt?

MOTHER: I don't know, darling.

GRANDFATHER: Of course you know, Marie. That yellow, François, is sulphur.

FRANÇOIS: *(Puzzled)* Sulphur?

MOTHER: Father, please.

GRANDFATHER: Sulphur is yellowish and smells bad, like hell. You understand?

FRANÇOIS: *(Unenlightened)* Like hell?

GRANDFATHER: When her sulphur shirt starts burning . . . *(Almost losing control of himself)* They've got to stage a guilty death for this girl! Now do you see?

MOTHER: Father! That's not the sort of thing to tell a child!

BERTRANDE: Heavens, no!

GRANDFATHER: You think not? Is it the sort of thing to let him watch?

MOTHER: Lord knows it isn't. But you're the one . . .

GRANDFATHER: *(Interrupting her)* It's not me, it's the times! It's the times that make him see things like that and it's my duty not to hide them from him! The times don't deserve anything better than those bastards down there! When a country . . .

AUDOUIN: Be quiet! She's going to pray. *(Pause)*

CATHERINE: Pray? In front of all those people?

AUDOUIN: In front of everybody. Out loud.

CATHERINE: Can you hear her?

AUDOUIN: No, it's too far.

CATHERINE: *(To herself)* I'd give my life to hear her voice. *(She walks slowly over to the window and gazes out.)* Oh, God! *(She falls to her knees. Pause. Her mother kneels beside her.)*

FRANÇOIS: Who's that man over there?

GILLES: Where? What man?

FRANÇOIS: The one behind her, in gray.

BERTHE: I see him! He just spit, is that the one?

FRANÇOIS: Yes. *(To Gilles)* Don't you see him?

GILLES: I see him, I see him.

FRANÇOIS: He has an iron bar in his hand.

GILLES: *(Curt)* I see him, I tell you.

FRANÇOIS: Don't get mad. *(Pause)*

GILLES: *(Expressionless)* I think it's time for me to go wake up Father.

GRANDFATHER: Why?

GILLES: He told me to.

GRANDFATHER: Let him sleep.

GILLES: That's not what he said.

GRANDFATHER: What do you think,

Marie? *(No answer)* Marie!

MOTHER: *(From the depths of her prayer)* Yes. *(She gets up, dazed.)* What is it?

GRANDFATHER: Your old man told Gilles to wake him up.

MOTHER: He'd better do it then.

GRANDFATHER: Do you think so?

MOTHER: When Jacques says to do something . . .

GRANDFATHER: *(Interrupting her)* Why should he want to see that?

MOTHER: Jacques doesn't confide in me.

(Noise from the crowd outside)

AUDOUIN: She's standing up now.

FRANÇOIS: Yes! And the gray man is walking over to her! *(The crowd gets louder.)* He's a giant!

MOTHER: Be quiet.

FRANÇOIS: He looks like a bear.

BERTRANDE: He does, doesn't he?

FRANÇOIS: A gray bear.

(The noise from outside gets still louder.)

BERTHE: Who is that man, Mama?

FRANÇOIS: He's looking at her. She's looking at him. He's taking hold of her arm!

CATHERINE: *(With a violent start)* No!

(Total silence in the square)

BERTHE: Who is he, Mama, who is he?

GRANDFATHER: *(Angry)* Child, are you a numbskull? He's the roaster!

BERTHE: *(Bewildered)* The . . . the roaster?

GRANDFATHER: A person who roasts.

FRANÇOIS: He's leading her away!

CATHERINE: No! No! No!

BERTHE: I think I'm a little scared . . .

MOTHER: I warned you.

AUDOUIN: *(Suddenly)* What does that mean? They're leaving.

GRANDFATHER: Who are?

AUDOUIN: The churchmen.

GRANDFATHER: The ones on the stage?

AUDOUIN: Yes, all of them. Archbishop, bishops, judges, they're all clearing out.

GRANDFATHER: The rats are abandoning ship.

BERTHE: Is it over?

MOTHER: Is what over?

BERTHE: The ceremony.

GRANDFATHER: Almost, my dear, almost.

BERTHE: Why are they all leaving?

GRANDFATHER: Because they're so soft-hearted.

ETIENNE: *(To Berthe, patiently)* Members of the clergy do not have the right to attend executions. You understand?

GRANDFATHER: She understands. There's more than one way to wash your hands of it.

GILLES: Look at the dust fly! All those capes and robes and cassocks sweeping around!

AUDOUIN: The wind's rising, had you noticed?

GRANDFATHER: Yes, I felt it blow across my face a minute ago. In a sense that's better.

FRANÇOIS: What do you mean?

GRANDFATHER: It'll go faster.

MOTHER: *(Jumps)* Oh!

GRANDFATHER: Do I shock you, Marie? We must be realistic, as Madame Maillard says. The sooner the girl is out of her misery, the better it'll be. *(Silence)*

CATHERINE: *(Barely audible)* Is there . . . much pain?

ETIENNE: Good lord!

BERTRANDE: I believe in being realistic up to a point. *(Pause)*

CATHERINE: Won't she be a little . . . dazed . . . overcome . . . by the smoke?

MOTHER: Don't think about that.

CATHERINE: That's all I *can* think about. I think about it so much I wonder if I'll ever be able to think about anything else. Burned, Mother, burned alive! *(Silence)*

GILLES: *(Speaking with difficulty)* One of the guards told me . . . *(He stops.)*

GRANDFATHER: Well, go on. What did he tell you?

GILLES: That it was horrible, that . . .

GRANDFATHER: Do you think you're helping things?

GILLES: He told me that the . . . executioner slips up and hits them on the head before the fire gets to them. He hits them with the iron rod that he stirs the fire with. He . . . he knocks them out.

CATHERINE: *(Close to tears)* Knocks them out?

GILLES: With a single blow. And they don't suffer.

CATHERINE: *(In agony)* Smashed with an iron rod — her beautiful head . . .

MOTHER: Don't think about it.

CATHERINE: Mother!

MOTHER: She's not thinking about it.

BERTRANDE: Hm-um.

MOTHER: No, she's not thinking about it. I know she's not. I'd swear she's not.

BERTRANDE: You don't even realize what's happening, you . . .

MOTHER: *(Interrupting her)* She's beyond thinking.

FRANÇOIS: *(In a shrill voice)* She's getting up on the logs!

GRANDFATHER: What?

FRANÇOIS: On the logs! She's going up!

GRANDFATHER: Is that true, Gilles?

GILLES: Yes.

GRANDFATHER: Already! *(He gets up.)*

FRANÇOIS: The gray man is going up with her. He's leading her by the hand.

CATHERINE: Mother, Mother!

MOTHER: Don't look.

FRANÇOIS: The monk is going up behind her! It's a long way up!

AUDOUIN: It must be as high as a house! Why did they drag in such a pile of wood?

GRANDFATHER: Is it *that* high?

AUDOUIN: It's huge. There's a forest of wood out there.

GRANDFATHER: As high as our window?

GILLES: Yes. I wonder why they . . . *(He stops.)*

GRANDFATHER: What do you wonder?

GILLES: Why they built such a mountain.

AUDOUIN: They must have had a reason. *(Pause)*

GRANDFATHER: Maybe Maillard knows.

ETIENNE: How should I know?

GRANDFATHER: You're a carpenter.

ETIENNE: So?

GRANDFATHER: You know about wood. By the way, there's none of your merchandise in this . . . display, I hope?

ETIENNE: *(Angry)* Are you serious?

FRANÇOIS: There she is! She's at the top!

BERTHE: What if she fell off!

BERTRANDE: It makes you dizzy.

AUDOUIN: I'm beginning to suspect something. Don't you imagine the height of that thing was calculated to . . .

FRANÇOIS: *(Interrupting him)* They're tying her to the stake!

ETIENNE: Don't shout like that!

FRANÇOIS: Look, look! The man is tying her to the stake!

ETIENNE: Shut up, I tell you!

CATHERINE: *(Mad with rage)* Why should he? Let him speak! Let him shout! Let her hear his voice! *(She rushes to the window.)*

BERTRANDE: *(Quickly to the Mother)* Don't let her do it, Madame Coutance!

CATHERINE: Let her hear a voice above the silence of this crowd! *(Standing directly in front of the window)* Yes, it's true. He's tying her up. I see him. I see him.

MOTHER: Control yourself, Catherine, please

CATHERINE: A horrible man who makes his living by killing people. He's touching her with his nasty hands, tying her arms, her legs, clamping an iron collar around her throat. It's a hideous sight, and these people are watching it. They're all watching, and nobody is saying a word.

MOTHER: You're making it worse for yourself, Catherine.

CATHERINE: *(Turning back toward the people in the room)* Nobody is saying a word. There are three hundred English sol-

diers, not even that many, two hundred, and ten thousand of us. If the ten thousand took one step, just one step forward, the two hundred would be swallowed up just like that, gone!

MOTHER: Catherine, don't torture yourself!

CATHERINE: But nobody is budging. Everybody is watching her suffer; everybody is watching her die, lashed to a stake like a wild beast. Everybody finds that normal, everybody thinks it's just fine! What's happening? *(Pause)* Speak up! Grandfather, what's happening? Is the world upside down?

GRANDFATHER: It is for a fact, my poor child. It's one of those moments when the world has gone mad.

CATHERINE: Nobody came to help her. Nobody will come. Nobody.

GRANDFATHER: I'm afraid not.

BERTRANDE: Who did you expect to come?

CATHERINE: I don't know . . . her soldiers . . . the ones from Orleans, from Reims, the ones that were with her when things were going well. Where are they? What are they doing? What about her old friends, LaHire, Dunois, all of them? What are they doing?

ETIENNE: You don't know what you're talking about. LaHire tried to get her out of the Rouen prison three weeks ago.

GRANDFATHER: That's a laugh!

ETIENNE: I swear he did.

GILLES: Who told you? Cabott?

ETIENNE: He wasn't the only one.

GRANDFATHER: So what happened?

ETIENNE: LaHire couldn't do it. It's not as easy as Catherine imagines.

CATHERINE: What about the king? The king of France? A man who owes her everything, everything from head to toe, from his crown to his spurs, what's the king of France doing? Playing cards? At Bourges? And what about her saints? Michael and Margaret? And Catherine, my patron saint? They were so chatty in the skies of Lorraine — does Normandy give them laryngitis? And what about God?

MOTHER: Be careful, Catherine.

CATHERINE: Is God watching the whole thing from his balcony? Just the way we are? It's unbelievable.

BERTRANDE: Were you expecting a miracle?

CATHERINE: I don't know, I was expecting . . . Isn't she a kind of miracle herself?

ETIENNE: That's just it.

CATHERINE: What do you mean?

ETIENNE: Miracles are short-lived and often work out wrong.

CATHERINE: Not like this, not like . . . like some savage ritual. *(She turns back to the window.)* My God, there's that hideous man going back down. He's finished. *(Pause)* She won't go down. Her feet will never touch the earth again. *(Silence)*

GRANDFATHER: *(Quietly)* What about the Dominican?

AUDOUIN: He's still up there, standing in front of her. He has his hands on her shoulders.

MOTHER: *(Her voice quavering)* Poor little shoulders . . . *(Pause. Someone shouts rudely from the square, "Hey, monk, come down!")*

GRANDFATHER: What was that?

GILLES: An English officer telling the monk to come down. *(Pause)*

GRANDFATHER: Is he doing it?

GILLES: No, he doesn't hear. *(The English soldier shouts again, louder this time, "Come down, you damned monk!" Pause)*

GRANDFATHER: He still doesn't hear?

GILLES: A soldier is going after him.

BERTHE: I'm scared, Mama.

BERTRANDE: Of course you are. *(To the Mother)* Don't you think the children should leave now?

FRANÇOIS: No, we want to see everything!

GILLES: You don't know what you're talking about.

FRANÇOIS: I do too. Gralin told me about it.

GILLES: About what? Who's Gralin?

FRANÇOIS: He's a friend. He saw somebody burned at Soissons last year and he told me all about it.

GILLES: Hearing is one thing and seeing is another. You won't be able to stand it.

FRANÇOIS: You want to bet?

GILLES: You're as white as a sheet.

AUDOUIN: The monk has come down. *(Silence)*

CATHERINE: *(Expressionless)* Now she's all alone. *(Anguished)* Oh, my God, do something! All alone, suspended.

GRANDFATHER: Isn't the wind rising?

AUDOUIN: Yes, more every minute.

CATHERINE: *(As if she hadn't been interrupted)* Suspended by wings . . . like a dove nailed to a tree. Oh, why can't she fly away, fly away! *(Pause)*

GILLES: *(Quietly)* There they go, they're lighting the fire.

MOTHER: *(Barely audible)* It's terrible, terrible . . .

AUDOUIN: *(Quietly)* The monk snatched the cross out of the procession leader's hand and he's holding it up toward her.

GILLES: *(Quietly)* They're having trouble, the wood won't catch.

GRANDFATHER: There's an east wind coming from Lorraine.

AUDOUIN: The monk is scrambling up the side of the logs. The English captain is having a fit, but the cross is rising higher and higher. Now it's even with Joan, right before her eyes.

GRANDFATHER: Maybe it'll hide everything else from her.

GILLES: The man that's trying to light the fire is squatting down with his back to the wind. Four English soldiers have formed a circle around him to shield the flame.

CATHERINE: She's afraid, I know she is. She's terrified. *(Raising her voice)* Joan, I'm with you!

GILLES: The four soldiers are standing back row and the man with the fire has stood up again.

CATHERINE: She's going to die of fear. Look at her — her mouth is open, she's screaming!

MOTHER: Oh, my God, please!

GILLES: *(Slowly, quietly)* The man is sticking the flame into a pile of dead weeds and grass under the logs.

(Total silence in the square and in the room)

FRANÇOIS: *(Suddenly, in a piercing voice)* Oh! Oh! Oh! The fire! *(A murmur surges up from the crowd, then silence again.)* It's like a snake, a great yellow snake creeping up on her . . .

BERTHE: *(In a high, little girl's voice)* The fire's started!

(Panic-stricken, the children rush to the door, out of the room and down the stairs, screaming in terror, "The fire! The fire!" In the room, everybody has turned away from the window except Catherine who is standing straight as a rod, staring out at the spectacle. It is as if she herself were tied to the stake.)

CATHERINE: It's not . . . it's not possible. Something is going to happen. Something is going to happen, just like that, a miracle. Oh God, make a miracle to put out the fire! Anything! Water, rain, a downpour, a flood, a deluge!

AUDOUIN: *(Turning around)* No flood could stop that fire now. The Seine could rush over it and it'd still burn.

CATHERINE: No, it wouldn't! It's just the grass and straw and kindling that's burning! The logs, the tree trunks, it'll take them a long time to catch! Won't it, Mother, won't it?

MOTHER: Yes, darling.

CATHERINE: Just think what a time we have lighting the stove!

ETIENNE: I'm sure they were careful what kind of logs they chose. They got dead ones, no doubt, dry as a bone . . .

CATHERINE: *(Interrupting him)* It's not all dead! Look! You can see blossoms on some of the branches!

ETIENNE: The wood on the bottom is

117

dry. They know what they're doing.

GRANDFATHER: Branches in blossom, are you sure? Are they apple blossoms?

ETIENNE: Yes, I think they are.

GRANDFATHER: Apple trees! The bastards!

CATHERINE: Oh God, the fire's still burning! It's spreading everywhere! Like a snake, he's right, a hideous yellow snake that slithers over the logs, wraps itself around the tree trunks and hisses, hisses! It's a hideous thing! *(She cries out.)* Joan, I'm with you!

MOTHER: *(Taking a step toward Catherine)* Catherine . . .

CATHERINE: Don't touch me! I'm not here, I'm out there with her! I'm in her — Joan, I'm inside you! I feel what you feel! All that you're suffering I suffer too! Oh my God, the fire is getting higher. It's closing in. I can't see her anymore! The cross!

AUDOUIN: The monk is holding his arms up as far as they'll go with the cross on the end of a stick. It's heavy.

CATHERINE: Hold the cross in front of my eyes! Dig the cross into my eyes!

AUDOUIN: The poor man is going to kill himself, mashed up against that fiery furnace.

CATHERINE: Blind me with the cross!

AUDOUIN: The monk's arms will surely be pulled out of their sockets. He looks crucified.

MOTHER: It's terrible, it's too terrible to be true.

GILLES: Look! The hem of the monk's habit is on fire! They're pulling him back. The cross has fallen.

CATHERINE: Where is it? Where is it? I can't see it anymore. I see an ocean of fire . . . a world of fire . . . the air is burning around me! I'm breathing fire!

AUDOUIN: What a bonfire! They're going to burn the whole town down.

CATHERINE: The cross! Where is the cross? The cross, like a cool spring, on my burning lips!

GILLES: The monk is lying on the ground, stretched out flat.

GRANDFATHER: Is he dead?

GILLES: No, he's praying.

CATHERINE: God! The smoke! The smoke, whipping in the wind, wrapping around me — I'm choking! *(She coughs.)* I'm choking, I'm choking! *(She coughs again.)*

BERTRANDE: Look! Look! *(A wisp of smoke comes in through the window.)*

GILLES: *(Quietly)* Grandfather, the smoke is coming in . . .

GRANDFATHER: Let it come in!

BERTRANDE: Don't you want to close the window?

GRANDFATHER: Close the window? Why?

BERTRANDE: The odor . . .

GRANDFATHER: It's the odor of martyrdom! Breathe it in! Breathe it in!

CATHERINE: Help! There's the fire! I can see it stealing up through the smoke! The fire, the fire is here! God, what unbearable heat! What an inhuman desert of flame and light! As if I'd been thrown into the eye of the sun!

MOTHER: *(In tears)* Have mercy on her!

ALL: *(Quietly)* Mercy!

(Smoke billows into the room. Bertrande coughs, then Gilles coughs.)

GRANDFATHER: Breathe it in! Breathe it in!

CATHERINE: (Panting) The fire is right in front of me! It's dancing! It hates me! Help! It's going to touch me!

MOTHER: Help!

ALL: Help!

CATHERINE: (With increasing frenzy) The blood is boiling in my veins! My skin is cracking! My eyes are dried out! (She cries out.) Oh! It's on me! My hair is on fire! I'm burning!

AUDOUIN: (At the window) A human torch.

CATHERINE: (Her voice still more piercing) I'm burning! I'm burning! (An almost inhuman cry) Jesus! (She falls to her knees. Long silence. Then Catherine speaks again, in a tender and faraway voice.) But my soul . . . my soul is like a fresh field of snow (She crumples to the floor.), new fallen snow. (Silence. No one moves. The smoke continues to come in through the window.)

GILLES: (Expressionless) Joan of Arc is dead.

AUDOUIN: (Also expressionless) Our Little Joan.

MOTHER: Pray for her. (She kneels.)

GRANDFATHER: Pray for yourself. You need it more than she does. (With the aid of his cane, he goes to the window and raises his blind eyes to the sky.) Good-bye, dear child, good-bye! (He bows his head.)

MOTHER: O Sancta Maria,
Mater alma Christi,
Carissima Maria . . .

BERTRANDE: Maria carissima . . . (She kneels.)

THE TWO WOMEN:
Suscipe pia Laudam praeconia nostra
Et nobis concedas venias per soecula
O Benigne! O Regina, O Maria!

GILLES AND AUDOUIN: O Maria! (They kneel.)

ALL FOUR: Te nunc flagitant devota corda et ora,
Nostra ut pura sint et pectora et corpora.

ETIENNE: Amen! (He kneels. Pause. Everyone remains kneeling, heads bowed, in silence.)

GRANDFATHER: (In a faraway voice) She's dead. But who knows what's just been born? (He goes slowly back to his chair.) What grandeur and glory this shameful fire will ignite in the world?
(Silence. Jacques Coutance, the Father, appears on the landing. He has on a baker's white work suit and is dusty with flour. He is a large and imperturbable man. He enters the room and stops. The Mother gets up quickly.)

COUTANCE: (Stating a fact, not a criticism) I had to comfort the little ones downstairs. I've never seen them like that. I thought they'd never stop crying.

MOTHER: (Still dazed) I know, Jacques, I'm sorry I let them . . .

COUTANCE: (Interrupting her gently) It wasn't your fault.

MOTHER: Catherine needed me, she . . .

COUTANCE: Of course she did. Don't

blame yourself, Marie. *(He walks calmly over to the window and closes it. Everyone but Catherine and the Grandfather stand up.)*

MOTHER: What are they doing?

COUTANCE: The children? They're playing in the courtyard, making crowns for each other out of chestnut blossoms.

BERTRANDE: *(Insensitive as usual)* Children are wonderful!

COUTANCE: That's what I thought when I was watching them laugh.

(Pause)

GILLES: I'm sorry I didn't come wake you up, Father.

COUTANCE: I wasn't asleep.

GILLES: Ah! *(Silence)*

BERTRANDE: Well, I guess we'd better be going.

ETIENNE: Yes, I hadn't realized we'd stayed so long.

BERTRANDE: It must be getting late. After a morning like this you wonder how you can go on. *(To Etienne)* Shall we go, love? *(To the others)* Thanks for taking us in.

ETIENNE: Yes, thanks again. See you later. *(They go to the door.)*

BERTRANDE: May I pick up my bread on the way out?

COUTANCE: Of course.

BERTRANDE: You can put it on my bill. Thanks again.

ETIENNE: Good-bye. *(They leave, closing the door after them.)*

BERTRANDE: I don't know *what* I can find for your lunch.

ETIENNE: It doesn't matter.

BERTRANDE: That's easy to say. *(The next exchange is heard as Bertrande and Etienne are going down the stairs.)* It's all well and good to call off the market, but people still have to eat.

ETIENNE: *(Concurring, almost inaudibly, as they close the outside door)* You can say that again.

GRANDFATHER: Whew! Glad *they're* gone!

AUDOUIN: Finally!

COUTANCE: Were they bad?

GILLES: You can't imagine.

COUTANCE: I think I can. *(He goes over to Catherine who is still prone. He looks at her tenderly.)* Time to get up, Catherine. *(Catherine sobs.)* Come on, little one. No more tears. *(He coaxes her up, holding her arm. She buries her face in his chest.)*

CATHERINE: Oh, Father, Father . . .

COUTANCE: I know, I know. *(He holds her against him.)* In this country, girls of twenty are brave and strong.

CATHERINE: *(In a quavering voice)* Yes, Father.

COUTANCE: That's a good girl. *(He strokes her hair.)* It seems to me you could do with a few days of fresh air away from the city.

GRANDFATHER: You're a wizard, son-in-law.

COUTANCE: I am? Why?

GRANDFATHER: I just gave your permission for Catherine to go home with Audouin this evening to Malaunay.

COUTANCE: Why this evening?

AUDOUIN: That's true. We could wait until tomorrow.

MOTHER: Don't you think this crowd of people . . .

CATHERINE: *(Showing signs of alarm)* Mother!

COUTANCE: What crowd? *(He glances toward the window.)* The beasts have gone back to their lairs. To digest their meal. To try to digest.

GRANDFATHER: I hope it sticks in their throats.

AUDOUIN: Let's go, Catherine!

MOTHER: But she doesn't have any clothes. I'll have to pack her a basket . . .

COUTANCE: No, stay here. *(To Audouin and Catherine)* Get going, you two!

MOTHER: My little girl! *(She takes Catherine in her arms.)*

COUTANCE: *(Separating them gently)* That's enough crying for one day. *(To the Mother)* We'll go pick her up on Sunday.

GILLES: That's a great idea!

MOTHER: To Malaunay?

COUTANCE: Why not? We'll leave at daybreak. We'll borrow the Maillards' new wagon. They owe us that much. *(To Audouin and Catherine)* Go on, you're losing time!

AUDOUIN: Good-bye.

CATHERINE: See you Sunday! *(They leave.)*

GRANDFATHER: You're a good man, son-in-law.

AUDOUIN: *(On the landing)* How do you feel?

CATHERINE: Strange. *(Catherine's next words are heard as she and Audouin go down the stairs.)* A little weak . . . all washed out and clean . . . all clean inside.

(Pause)

COUTANCE: Did she suffer?

MOTHER: Catherine? Terribly.

GRANDFATHER: But not as much as the other one.

COUTANCE: No . . . What cruelty. *(He goes to the window, glances around the square and shudders.)* What stupid cruelty!

GRANDFATHER: I'm going to tell you something . . . *(He is interrupted by a sound of voices outside. Then someone knocks vigorously on the shop door downstairs.)*

MOTHER: *(Startled)* Who could that be?

COUTANCE: Can't you imagine? Hm! They're hungry now. The ordeal wore them out. *(He looks out the window at the people in front of his shop.)* Look at that line. *(To Gilles)* Go open the shop.

GILLES: Yes, Father. *(He goes to the door.)*

MOTHER: I'll go too. *(They go out, leaving the door open.)*

COUTANCE: And don't let them push. Line them up.

MOTHER: *(On the landing)* All right, Jacques.

GILLES: Don't worry, Father. *(They go down the stairs. Voices outside, fists banging on the shop door.)*

COUTANCE: *(Speaking toward the window)* Stop shouting! Don't kick my door with your filthy feet! *(To the Grandfather)* I'd like to swat their hands off my clean bread. I'd better go down and help. *(He heads to the door.)*

GRANDFATHER: Listen, baker. *(Cou-*

121

tance stops.) I'm going to tell you something. *(Coutance turns around on the threshold.)* Something that it's taken me all my life to learn. *(He gets up and goes over to his son-in-law, looking at him with blank eyes.)* For rich people, for nobles, for . . . for politicians, there isn't any good and evil. You follow me?

COUTANCE: I follow you.

GRANDFATHER: They're above all that. But for the little man like us, my son, a crime is a crime.

COUTANCE: And crime is punished.

GRANDFATHER: *(His face lighting up)* I see that you follow me. Conclusion, baker: the bastards have had it.

COUTANCE: I think so too. *(He goes out laughing, clattering down the stairs. Alone, the Grandfather crosses almost jauntily to the window, opens it wide and as the curtain falls, shouts out into the square.)*

GRANDFATHER: You've had it.

curtain

André Obey

(1892-1975)

When André Obey died in April 1975, his devotion to the theatre was undiminished. His last full-length play *(Le Jour du retour The Reunion,* in this volume, originally called *Les Retrouvailles)* was followed by two one-acts in the early 1970's: *Le Bibliothécaire* and *La Nuit des chevaux.*

As a lifelong disciple of Jacques Copeau, Obey is in the distinguished company of Valentine Tessier, Georges and Ludmilla Pitoëff, Gaston Baty, Charles Dullin, Louis Jouvet, André Gide, Jean Giraudoux, Jean Vilar, Jean-Louis Barrault, Madeleine Renaud. Copeau's and Obey's principles of drama can hardly be separated a scrupulous regard for the written text, a sense of the theatre as vocation, a preference for the classics and classical themes, and an asceticism in discipline and production that has led to a sometimes dangerous disregard for commercial success. The two men's somewhat solitary, pensive inclinations, and their preference for a simple rural life, also happened to coincide.

As playwright, adaptor, director, and musician, Obey was a versatile talent. In addition to about thirty original plays, he has written many adaptations, including two from Shakespeare, *Richard III* and *Henri IV; Maria,* a play-within-a-play based on Faulkner's short story "Mistral"; an *Oedipus Tyrannus* from Sophocles; an adaptation of the *Oresteia* written at the request of Barrault who played the role of Orestes; an immensely successful French version of Tennessee Williams' *Cat on a Hot Tin Roof;* a stage play based on the television script of *Twelve Angry Men.* At the end of World War II, Obey directed the dramatic and literary programs of *Radio-diffusion Française,* after which he spent two years as director of the Comédie-Française. His deep interest in music dates back to his childhood in Douai where he won first prize in piano at the conservatory of music.

Obey's mode, the neo-classical, is now in the downswing of the eternal cycle of public taste. The dramatic qualities of his plays, however, assure him a revival when the time is right.

— JDS

THIS BOOK WAS DESIGNED BY
JUDITH M. OELFKE
PRINTED IN NINE POINT HELVETICA LIGHT
ON WARREN'S LUSTRO ENAMEL DULL BOOK
BY MOTHERAL PRINTING COMPANY
AND BOUND BY
JOHN D. ELLIS BINDERY

1380